VILLA

MILITARY PROFILES
SERIES EDITOR
Dennis E. Showalter, Ph.D.
Colorado College

*Instructive summaries for general and expert
readers alike, volumes in the Military Profiles
series are essential treatments of significant and
popular military figures drawn from world history,
ancient times through the present.*

VILLA

Soldier of the Mexican Revolution

Robert L. Scheina

Brassey's, Inc.
Washington, D.C.

Published in the United States by Brassey's, Inc. All rights reserved. No part
of this book may be reproduced in any manner whatsoever without written
permission from the publisher, except in the case of brief quotations embodied
in critical articles and reviews.

Library of Congress Cataloging-in-Publication Data

Scheina, Robert L.
Villa : Soldier of the Mexican Revolution / Robert L. Scheina.
    p. cm. — (Military profiles)
  Includes bibliographical references and index.
  ISBN 1-57488-513-8 (alk. paper) — ISBN 1-57488-662-2
  1. Villa, Pancho, 1878-1923—Military leadership.   2.
  Mexico—History—Revolution, 1910-1920—Campaigns.   3. Divisiâon del
Norte (Mexico)   I. Title. II. Series.
F1234.V63S34 2004
972.08'1'092—dc22   2003028042

Hardcover ISBN 1-57488-513-8
Softcover ISBN 1-57488-662-2

Printed in the United States of America on acid-free paper that meets the
American National Standards Institute z39-48 Standard.

Brassey's, Inc.
22841 Quicksilver Drive
Dulles, Virginia 20166

FIRST EDITION

10 9 8 7 6 5 4 3 2 1

Contents

Preface and Acknowledgments

Pancho Villa was a true *caudillo*, toughest of the tough, a generous patron to those who followed him loyally, and a terrifying enemy. He was born into violence, routinely dispensed violence, and died violently.

Pancho Villa possessed many contradistinctions. He befriended and protected murderers and social do-gooders with equal enthusiasm. He executed many while forgiving others. During his early years, he rarely drank or cursed but frequently robbed and murdered. These contradistinctions made him easy to hate if you chose to ignore his benevolences, and easy to love if you decided to overlook his vices. But we can do neither.

Numerous biographies of Pancho Villa exist, so why write one more? This book answers the question, how good a military commander was this man who led tens of thousands of fighters but is most frequently remembered as a bloodthirsty bandit. This book is all about how Villa won and lost on the battlefield.

Throughout the book, I have cited the distance ("as the crow flies") and direction of important geographical locations from a central one, most often Mexico City; for example, "Chihuahua City (800 miles northwest of Mexico City)." I do this to convey to the reader an appreciation of the vast distances over which Pancho Villa campaigned.

Many scholars who have devoted much of their lives to the study of Mexico have helped me. As in the past, I would be grossly remiss if I did not thank my two mentors, to whom I was a challenge: Dr. Richard Greenleaf and the late Father Antonine

Tibesar. Next, to my very good friend Dr. Barbara Tenenbaum, the Mexican specialist at the Hispanic-American Division, Library of Congress, thank you for your never-ending help. I want to thank Mr. John Klingemann of Sul Ross University, Texas, for his help in providing regional insights. Two prominent citizens of the city of Chihuahua helped by generously sharing resources, Dr. Rubén Osorio and *Licenciado* Miguel Maldonado Olivas. I would also like to thank Ms. Terri Grant of the Border Heritage Center, El Paso Public Library, for extensive help with the photography.

For thirty-six years, my wife, Linda, has never lessened her encouragement of my writing. This is very greatly appreciated. To my agent, Fritz Heinzen, thank you for yet another opportunity.

The views expressed in this book are those of the author and do not reflect the official policy or position of the National Defense University, the Department of Defense, or the U.S. Government.

Maps

Chronology

circa 1878	Pancho Villa is born as Doroteo Arango.
1910	On November 17, Abraham González, the leader of the anti–Porfirio Díaz movement in Chihuahua, sends his bodyguard, which includes Pancho Villa, into the mountains to gather fighters.
1911	On May 10, the Maderistas, including Villa, capture Ciudad Juárez and the Porfirio Díaz government collapses.
	On November 16, Francisco Madero is elected president of Mexico while Villa operates a butcher shop in Chihuahua City.
1912	On March 4, Pascual Orozco rebels against President Madero, and Villa raises a guerrilla force to fight Orozco.
	On June 4, General Victoriano Huerta, whom Madero sent to fight Orozco, arrests Pancho Villa and orders him shot. Villa is held in various prisons in Mexico City before escaping.
1913	On February 22, General Victoriano Huerta assassinates President Madero and Vice President José Pino Suárez and seizes the government. Villa, who had escaped to the United States, recrosses the border to fight the usurper, Huerta.
	On September 29, after winning numerous skirmishes, Villa is chosen to lead the Division of the North, a confederation of irregular cavalry bands led by *caudillos.*

On October 1, Villa captures Torreón, but is forced to abandon it to secure his base of support.

On November 15, Villa captures the border town Ciudad Juárez in a surprise attack.

On November 24 and 25, he crushes the Huertistas at Tierra Blanca.

In December, he seizes the governorship of Chihuahua.

1914　In early January, Pancho Villa drives the Huertista defenders at Ojinaga into the United States and internment. Artillery expert General Felipe Angeles joins Villa's Division of the North and transforms it from an irregular cavalry to a disciplined army.

On February 17, Villa orders his chief assassin, Rodolfo Fierro, to kill Scotsman William Benton. In March, Pancho Villa meets Venustiano Carranza for the first time, but dislikes him.

Between March 22 and April 2, Villa captures a well-defended Torreón for the second time.

On April 15, Villa defeats the Huertistas at San Pedro.

On April 21 the U.S. Navy seizes Veracruz, Mexico.

On May 17, Venustiano Carranza insists that Pancho Villa attack the Huertistas at Paredón. Villa does, and wins.

On June 17, against Venustiano's wishes, Villa attacks and defeats Huertistas at Zacatecas, opening the way to Mexico City.

On July 15, Huerta resigns as president of Mexico.

In August or September, Villa and Alvaro Obregón meet in northern Mexico to try to resolve their differences.

On November 1, the Aguascalientes Convention elects Eulalio Gutiérrez as interim president.

On December 4, Villa and Emiliano Zapata meet for the first time. Two days later, 50,000 Villistas and Zapatistas parade together through Mexico City.

1915   On January 5, General Felipe Angeles defeats Carrancistas at Ramos Arizpe and occupies Monterrey.

Between April 6 and 7, and 13 and 15, respectively, Villa is defeated by Alvaro Obregón at the First and Second Battles of Celaya.

Between April 27 and June 6, Villa loses a series of battles to Obregón, the most important being Trinidad.

On July 10, Villa is again defeated, this time at Aguascalientes.

On September 11, artillery expert and organizer Felipe Angeles leaves Villa and goes to the United States.

Between November 1 and 3, Villa is defeated at Agua Prieta by General Plutarco Calles, who is helped by the United States.

On November 22, Villa is defeated at Hermosillo.

1916   On January 19, Villistas stop a train near Santa Isabel, Chihuahua and execute seventeen Americans.

On March 9, Villa's force raids Columbus, New Mexico, killing eighteen Americans.

On March 15, the 6,000-man Pershing Expedition enters Mexico, but Villa eludes the Americans.

On September 16, Villa surprises and captures Chihuahua City.

On December 22, he takes Torreón for the third and final time.

1917   On May 30, Villa again drives the garrison of Ojinaga across the border into the United States.

1919   On April 19, Villa attacks and captures the town of
              Hidalgo del Parral, with Felipe Angeles once again
              at his side.

                  On June 14, Villa attacks Ciudad Juárez, but
              U.S. artillery fires on his forces from El Paso, Texas,
              and American troops cross the border and drive
              him off.

                  On November 26, Felipe Angeles is executed by
              the Carranza government after having, once again,
              deserted Villa.

1920   On July 28, Villa surrenders to the de la Huerta
              government and agrees to retire.

1923   Pancho Villa is assassinated on July 20 in Parral.

VILLA

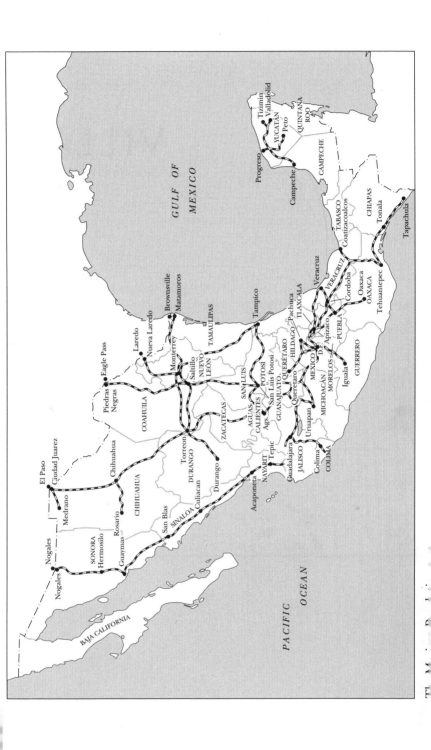

The Main Rail Lines of Mexico

Chapter 1

Fighting "The Old Establishment," 1887–1912

S ONORA, CHIHUAHUA, AND COAHUILA—the Mexican states that border the southwestern United States—had always been the Mexican "badlands." Ever since the days of the Spanish conquest during the sixteenth century, this is where the civilized crashed into the uncivilized. Yaqui and Apache Indians rampaged, and outlaws plundered. Deprivation was the norm, and death was too often brutal.

A new order began to permeate the territory in the waning decades of the nineteenth century; although more subtle, it was just as brutal and unjust. President José de la Cruz Porfirio Díaz, *el máximo caudillo* (the ultimate leader), extended his brand of justice from the capital of Mexico. This new order was the exploitation of the wealth—mostly cattle, cotton, and min-ing—by and for the benefit of Don Porfirio's friends. Open range was titled to the elite, wild cattle were rounded up and branded by the new landholders, and great haciendas were built where maids wearing Parisian uniforms served *every* need of their employers. Those who broke the rules were hunted down by the *rurales* (federal police) and frequently killed "while trying to escape" (*matalos en caliente*).[1]

Into this harsh reality rode Pancho Villa, a man who became a legend. Though it is much easier to document the myth than to find the reality, it is the truth we seek.

Francisco Villa was born Doroteo Arango in 1878, the illegitimate son of Don Luis Fermán, a wealthy *hacendado* (landholder) who had had an affair with his maid. Doroteo was the eldest of five children and, to stave off starvation, went to work at El Gorgojito ranch, which belonged to the López Negrete family. According to legend, the owner, López's son, and the foreman tried to rape Martina, Doroteo's sister, one of the perks of the wealthy. However, since Villa's sister would have been an infant at that time, the rape story is improbable. But for whatever reason, Doroteo shot someone, either the son of the owner or a *rurales* officer; accounts do not agree. He fled into the countryside and was caught, killed one of his guards, and escaped.[2]

Around 1891, he turned to banditry. During the next twenty years, Doroteo alternated between being a bandit and a cattle butcher. Which was his vocation and which was his avocation are not altogether clear. The dispositions of authors toward Doroteo are captured in their explanation of how he chose his new name. Sympathetic Ramón Puente, who worked as his secretary, explained that Doroteo chose the name Francisco Villa to return to the legitimacy of his grandfather. On the other hand, unsympathetic Jessie Peterson and Thelma Knoles state that Doroteo selected the name to honor an early nineteenth-century bandit.[3]

How many crimes Pancho Villa committed during these twenty years is anyone's guess. Surely and frequently, he killed, stole, kidnapped, and committed arson. He abducted Petra Espinosa and then married her. In fact, he would "honor" many women by marrying them only to abandon them after a short period of time. In 1909 he burned down the town hall of Rosario. The celebrated journalist, John Reed, wrote, "His misdeeds have no parallel with those of any other celebrated person in the world."[4]

But what about his qualities? At the very least Pancho Villa was disturbed by the injustices that surrounded him and increasingly became a self-appointed avenger.

In 1910 Pancho Villa met with Abraham González, who led the political campaign in Chihuahua to prevent José de la Cruz Porfirio Díaz from being reelected president of Mexico. It was dangerous for a "reputable" bandit to confer with an "irresponsible" idealist—such meetings bred revolution. For Porfirio Díaz, in his thirty-fifth year of dictatorship, had every intention of being reelected—regardless of what it might take. In July, Claro Reza, who had ridden in Villa's gang, denounced Pancho's political awakening to the authorities. Not one to accept betrayal forgivingly, Villa murdered Claro. Writers do not agree on where and how Villa killed him, but they do agree that Villa did it in person.[5]

Francisco Madero, the anti-reelection candidate, fled to Texas in early October dressed as a mechanic after losing a rigged presidential election in which the votes were counted by the victor, Porfirio Díaz. Madero denounced the reelection of the dictator from the safety of San Antonio. He called for his countrymen to take up arms on November 20 and overthrow the old dictator.[6]

In 1910 President Porfirio Díaz was at the height of his prestige internationally. He had made Mexico "the mother of the foreigner and stepmother of the Mexican." The "love affair" that foreigners had with Don Porfirio was captured by George W. Crichfield in his book, *American Supremacy*. He wrote: "This great man, by reason of his marvelous genius and achievements, is entitled to rank at the head of all rulers and statesmen which Latin America has produced."[7] Díaz' sources of power were the elites, the army, and the federal police, all of whom Pancho Villa hated.[8]

Three "Mexicos" existed in 1910. There was the U.S.-oriented north where disenfranchised cowboys (*vaqueros*) worked the range for their masters, the European-oriented cities of the central valley where the proletariat struggled to enter the industrial world, and the Indian-oriented south where most still lived in feudal-like bondage. Villa was from the world of the cowboy and prior to the 1910 election had no knowledge of the other two Mexicos. Mexico's population in 1910 was almost twelve million inhabitants. Of these, only 195,000 were laborers, 500,000 were artisans and intellectuals, and 11-plus million were peasants.[9]

The myth of the Mexican army was captured by Thomas Janvier: "The Mexican army is an honor to the government that has created it, and affords the surest guarantee that in Mexico the days of revolutions are ended, and that the existing constitutional government will endure."[10]

The truth of the Mexican army was that it was top-heavy with officers—nine thousand—commanding some eighteen thousand men. Most of the soldiers were forced into service by press gangs, a system known as *la leva*. Most senior officers held their rank thanks to their old friend Porfirio Díaz and they themselves were old—too old to lead a physically demanding campaign in the field. True, the Chapultepec Military School was graduating well-trained young officers, and these graduates represented about half of the junior officers. The twenty-seven states of Mexico were divided into eleven military districts. Don Porfirio switched district commanders and state governors on short notice to inhibit them from winning local followings.

Porfirio Díaz tolerated corruption by senior officers in order to ensure their loyalty. General Manuel Mondragón, chief of artillery, personally received half a cent on every rifle cartridge manufactured in Mexico even if they would not fire properly. Finance Minister José Limantour worked to prevent promiscuous stealing by the high army officers but he had only limited success.[11]

The Mexican Revolution began like an old, cold steam engine, coughing and sputtering, as it worked to build pressure, first in northern Mexico and then in the central and southern states. The number of rebels committed to fight for Madero was less important than the number who had guns; frequently that was the deciding factor in how many rebels showed up for a fight.[12]

Among these soon-to-be revolutionaries was Francisco Villa. On October 4, Villa and fifteen other men began protecting the home of Abraham González, the local Maderista political chief. On November 17, González sent his bodyguards, including Villa, south to recruit fighters. The 375 new revolutionaries captured the hamlets of San Andrés and nearby Santa Isabel without a fight on November 22 Next Villa, leading a handful of men, foolishly attacked a federal force of some eight hundred soldiers led by General Juan Navarro and was lucky to escape with just a minor leg wound.[13]

Far away in Mexico City, Porfirio Díaz did not immediately perceive the severity of the threat presented by the Madero-led revolution. Once he did, he was reluctant to commit his entire army against the rebels for fear that the outside world would lose confidence in his government. Besides, almost half of the army was already garrisoned in the northern states, which were chronically plagued by bandits, Indians, anarchists, and dissidents.[14]

Initially, the insurgents had no strategy, only a goal, and that was to overthrow Porfirio Díaz. This was the glue that held their diverse fraternity together. Because no central control existed, numerous uncoordinated acts of rebellion broke out throughout Mexico.[15]

Back in the state of Chihuahua in northern Mexico, the insurgents began evolving from hit-and-run guerrillas into a feudal-like army where the fighters owed allegiance to their *caudillo,* who in turn gave his to Francisco Madero. On November 21, Madero crossed the Rio Grande River back into Mexico; he lost his way and found a mere twenty men waiting to support him, only half of whom were armed. Disillusioned and believing that the rebellion was a failure, he recrossed into the United States. Madero considered giving up the revolution and seeking safety in Europe from Don Porfirio's long reach.[16]

However, on that same day, Pascual Orozco, a muleteer leading fewer than thirty followers, emerged as the first *caudillo* to rise above his revolutionary brethren. He captured the town of Guerrero (60 miles west-southwest of Chihuahua City and 800 miles northwest of Mexico City) from more than sixty federal soldiers. He executed the federal officers and government officials. Orozco gave the captured soldiers a choice—join his army or be shot. This became the standard recruiting practice by all factions throughout the ten years of revolution. Orozco also sent a telegram to Pancho Villa in San Andrés, "Come and I will give you some ammunition."[17] Three days later, Villa arrived and found that Orozco and the local population had embraced revolutionary ideals.[18]

A number of revolutionary bands, including that led by Villa, joined Orozco. On December 11, they fought a meeting engagement (both forces on the march) near the village of Cerro Prieto and sustained heavy casualties. The revolutionaries retreated into the mountains, and Navarro executed twenty-two villagers, including the old and young.[19]

The revolution continued to spread throughout Mexico. Villa returned from the mountains leading five hundred *vaqueros* (cowboys) and, beginning in December, fought a number of minor skirmishes, sometimes besting the federal troops. On February 7, 1911, Villa captured Ciudad Camargo (Santa Rosalía), eighty miles southeast of Chihuahua City (700 miles northwest of Mexico City).[20]

On February 14, Madero again crossed into Mexico from the United States, this time with the American authorities in hot pursuit. The authorities wanted to charge him, a Mexican, under an antifilibustering law that prohibited armed expeditions launched from the United States against other nations. The irony of this is that historically this law was rarely enforced against Americans leading expeditions against Latin American nations.[21]

It is unclear when Villa first met Francisco Madero, but according to Villa's diary, the meeting took place at about this time. This 5'2" well-to-do rancher, who had anointed himself the champion of those who opposed the dictator, captivated Villa. Madero, in priestly fashion, forgave Villa his past and accepted him into the movement.[22]

Madero's presence provided political legitimacy to the rebellion and boosted morale, but it was Orozco's initiatives that determined the military strategy. Orozco cut the rail line between Chihuahua City (800 miles northwest of Mexico City) and Ciudad Juárez. If the rebels could take this border town, they would have a base of operations and could import arms from the United States. Led by Madero, the rebels occupied Zaragoza, Chihuahua, some ten miles southeast of Ciudad Juárez (1,221 miles northwest of Mexico City) without a fight.[23]

Next Madero attacked Casas Grandes at two o'clock in the morning on March 6 with eight hundred ill-equipped men. After four hours of heavy fighting, the defenders, five hundred men from the eighteenth Infantry Battalion, ran up the white flag. Victory appeared to be at hand and some of the Maderistas advanced to accept the surrender. But the defenders were rescued by the arrival of federal troops commanded by Samuel García Cuéllar, chief of the Presidential General Staff (*Jefe del Estado Mayor Presidencial*). The Maderistas were driven off. A company of American volunteers fighting for the rebels sustained particularly heavy casualties. Madero lost most of his supplies, and he was slightly wounded. He recrossed the Río Grande and took on tasks more suited to his skills: giving speeches and raising money.[24]

On March 12, other Maderistas were defeated at Cerro Prieto, but they did capture a machine gun—their first. A few days later, the Maderistas drove the federal troops out of Agua Prieta, the sister border town to Douglas, Arizona. In spite of these ups and downs, volunteers poured into Madero's camp. These fighters swelled the rebel army to three thousand men in the north, where they were led by Pascual Orozco and Pancho Villa, the men who for the most part had gathered them. Throughout Mexico, the revolutionaries were experiencing increasing success.[25]

Porfirio Díaz began to appreciate the gravity of the threat. He rushed troops north. But his army, built on patronage and corruption, was not up to the fight. Officers with loaded revolvers stood in the doorways of the railroad cars to keep the forcibly-conscripted soldiers from deserting. And the soldiers who did get to fight were often given faulty ammunition that had been purchased at great discount—and at great profit by the acquisition agents.[26]

The three thousand Maderistas (or perhaps more accurately, Orozquistas and Villistas) now advanced against Ciudad Juárez. The city was the site of an important customs house, which was defended by some five hundred well-fortified federal troops. It turned out to be a "fashionable" fight, attracting the notable adventurers of the world. Among the Maderistas were about one hundred "foreign legionaries" who included Giuseppe Garibaldi (grandson of the Italian revolutionary), Ben Viljoen (a former Boer War general), A. W. Lewis (a machine gun inventor), Lou Carpentier (a French artilleryman), Sam Dreben (noted soldier of fortune), Oscar Creighton ("The Dynamite Devil"), and Tom Mix (future movie star).[27]

Madero once again crossed the border. But he soon became concerned that attacking Ciudad Juárez might result in stray shells falling into El Paso on the American side of the border and inadvertently cause U.S. intervention. So Madero decided not to attack Ciudad Juárez but rather to march to Mexico City and negotiate with the old dictator. This Pollyanna scheme bewildered Orozco and Villa.[28]

Neither Orozco nor Villa was willing to accept what they believed to be an illogical military decision, so they concocted a scheme to bring on a general engagement. Villa later wrote (because as yet, he had not learned how): "We contrived to launch our attack by military logic, circumventing Sr. Madero. . . . Sometimes a civilian chief is unable to see what is plain to the eyes of his military subordinate. If the success of . . . a revolution is at stake, that subordinate must be guided by his own judgment."[29]

Orozco and Villa sent fifteen men toward Ciudad Juárez with orders to start a fight. Then Orozco and Villa sent fifty more "to rescue" them. More followed to rescue the fifty. Madero rushed toward the sound of the shooting in order to stop the fighting, but his horse was shot from under him. Before long, Orozco and Villa had their general engagement: three thousand irregulars against the five-hundred-man garrison.[30]

The fighting began on May 8 and raged through the tenth. Although, on paper, the federal garrison was commanded by eighty-year-old General Juan Navarro, a connoisseur of cognac, in fact it was led by Colonel Manuel Tamborell, a graduate of the Chapultepec Military School. He had prepared the defenses well. The defenders were armed with machine guns and French-manufactured mortars. Rifle pits were dug for the outer defenses, and the streets were barricaded between the buildings on the edge of town to form the inner defenses. Capturing such a fortified town seemed like an impossible task for an attacking force that possessed almost no artillery.[31]

And the Maderista artillery was truly pitiful—all of two guns. One was an American Civil War Napoleon that had been stolen from in front of the city hall of El Paso, Texas, and towed across the shallow Rio Grande. Its shells were manufactured in the United States and smuggled across the river. The second gun was a homemade cannon. After the melee started, these two guns, commanded by the Frenchman Carpentier, joined in. The second shot miraculously took out the water tank at the federal barracks. Unfortunately, instead of firing forward, the homemade weapon then blew its breech-block backward, which destroyed the gun.[32]

Newspaperman John Turner described the battle:

They [the Maderistas] moved in no formation whatsoever, just an irregular stream of them. . . . They would fight awhile and then come back to rest, sleep, and eat, returning refreshed to the front.

The European-trained soldiers raved at this, tried to turn them back. . . . But that was not the way of these chaps from Chihuahua. They knew their business and they knew it well.

That casual way of fighting, I think, more than any other one thing, took Juárez. For by it the *insurrectos* [insurgents] were always fresh, with high spirits, while the little brown federals with no sleep and little food or water, with their officers behind them ready with their pistols to kill quitters, soon lost their morale.[33]

Once the Maderistas reached the edge of town, they dynamited their way through the walls of the connected buildings, thus bypassing the federal street barricades. Following three days of hard fighting, the federal troops, low on ammunition, surrendered. The federals lost one hundred eighty dead, including Colonel Tamborrell, and two hundred fifty wounded. Casualties among the Maderistas were surely higher, but apparently no one counted.[34]

Among those Villa captured was General Juan Navarro. Orozco reminded Villa that Navarro had executed not only rebel prisoners but also those merely suspected of being Maderistas. He proposed that Navarro be shot whether Madero agreed with them or not. Villa was probably not hard to convince. However, when the idea of shooting Navarro was presented to Madero, Orozco intimated that it was Villa's idea. Although not a soldier, Madero was a brave man who rescued Navarro and permitted him to escape. Villa was so outraged that he pointed his pistol at Madero, but Madero, showing great courage, told Villa, "If you dare to kill me, shoot!" Villa broke down and embraced him, saying, "I have committed a black infamy."[35]

On May 17, the two sides signed a five-day truce that proved to be the death-knell of the Porfiriato (the Porfirio Díaz regime). The capture of Ciudad Juárez gave the rebels access to arms and munitions from the United States. The aging Díaz had failed to send adequate forces against the *insurgentes* in the north. More important, this insurgent victory demonstrated that the federal army was not invincible. The elites forced the aging dictator to resign and had congress select an interim president in an effort to reestablish economic order.[36]

Orozco and Villa had led their men to victory. Formal military academies might dispute the fact that Orozco and Villa provided true generalship since they succeeded by continually risking their lives while paying little attention to strategy and tactics. Nevertheless, the fighters (for surely using the term *soldiers* is too formal) were there because Orozco and Villa had brought them, and they remained there because they believed that Orozco and Villa would lead them to victory and reward them for their sacrifices. Orozco and Villa held their trust.

The Navarro incident soured the relationship between Madero and his two victorious *caudillos*. However, Villa almost immediately forgot about the disagreement. He returned to Chihuahua City, married his sweetheart, María Luz Corral (who would outlast all his other wives and fall heiress to his wealth), and opened a butcher shop with the fifteen thousand pesos that he had received in compensation for his services. Villa emerged from this first phase of the Mexican Revolution as an individual of whom the major power brokers needed to keep track and court.

But Orozco, whose role had earned him a more prominent status than Villa's, was not so willing to reconcile his differences with Madero. Orozco had been given one hundred thousand pesos as campaign expenses and the command of troops in Chihuahua. This was not enough. Orozco wanted to be appointed to Madero's cabinet and given a much larger payment, for, after all, he was the key architect of Madero's victory at Ciudad Juárez, which had given Madero the presidency.[37]

Chapter 2

Fighting Orozco, 1912–13

ON JUNE 6, 1911, Francisco Madero tri-
umphantly entered Mexico City and was elected president on
November 6. Surprisingly, it had taken very little time and blood
to oust the once-invincible dictator of 36 years. Almost immediately, some disturbing new realities emerged. First, the glue—
opposition to Porfirio Díaz—that had bonded the disparate
revolutionaries to Madero was gone. Rebellious *caudillos* pressed
for the adoption of their regional agendas. Some now perceived
Madero as the establishment; he had gone from being the solution to becoming the problem. Second, the Porfiriato army, the
tool of the elite, had not really been defeated. Rather, the old
dictator had reluctantly quit the fight. Rebellions against
Madero very quickly exploded and were led by some dissatisfied
new power brokers, the *caudillos*, and the undefeated old elite.
Revolutionaries Emiliano Zapata and Pascual Orozoco and elit-
ists Bernardo Reyes and Féliz Díaz all rebelled.[1]

The Zapata brothers led a rebellion in the poor, small state of
Morelos, just to the south of Mexico City, where huge sugar
plantations owned by absentee landlords had squeezed out the

centuries-old communal lands (*ejidos*). Madero was forced to use the Porfiriato army to prevent Zapata from redistributing land at gunpoint. The army was able to seize the towns, but Zapata held the countryside.[2]

Next, General Bernardo Reyes rebelled. Toward the end of the Porfiriato, Reyes was frequently perceived to be the old dictator's successor. On December 4, 1911, Reyes secretly crossed into San Antonio, Texas, where he purchased arms. The U.S. Government discovered his activities and seized his cache. Reyes escaped to Matamoros on December 13. After a skirmish between Reyes and troops loyal to Madero, Reyes surrendered at Linares, Nuevo León, on December 25. General Reyes was brought to Mexico City and imprisoned at the Santiago Tlaltelolco Military Prison. Although sentenced to death, Reyes was spared when Madero commuted his punishment. There in prison in the near future, the lives of General Reyes and Pancho Villa would cross.[3]

Pascual Orozco was the third major figure to rebel against Madero, doing so on March 4, 1912. Orozco was motivated by the belief that he had not been adequately rewarded for his services in defeating Porfirio Díaz, by a personal dislike of Madero, and by the prodding of the super-rich Terrazas family which still dominated Chihuahua. Orozco urged Pancho Villa to join him against Madero, but Villa would not betray the president. Villa possessed a deep respect for Madero and a deep hatred for Orozco, believing that he had attempted to use him in the Navarro affair.[4]

Villa was the first to take the field of battle against Orozco. Villa slipped out of Chihuahua City and began gathering a following. Unlike Orozco, he had no rich backers. Leading five hundred horsemen, Villa appeared before the mining town of Parral (125 miles south-southeast of Chihuahua City) on March 19. He sent the following ultimatum, "If you are loyal to the government [of Madero], come out to receive me, and if you are an enemy, come out to fight. I shall take the town in any case. Francisco Villa."[5] The garrison chose not to fight and Villa occupied Parral. On the following day, Orozquistas attacked the town but were driven off. They returned three days later in greater strength, and Villa abandoned Parral, but not before collecting a "loan" from the leading citizens.[6]

During the Villista retreat, the Orozquistas captured the America soldier of fortune, machine gunner Tom Fountain. He was shot "while trying to escape" (*matalos en caliente*). But those who were first tortured by the Orozquistas envied those who died quickly. Villa avenged these acts as frequently as he could by shooting all captured Orozquistas. Villa never possessed enough strength to directly challenge Orozco so he captured small towns, seized any items of value, and then disappeared.[7]

While Villa was raiding the small towns, the Madero government sent Secretary of War General José González Salas, leading primarily militiamen, to fight Orozco's seasoned followers; Orozco's men were known as *Colorados* by the Mexicans and "Red Flaggers" by the Americans because of the red hatbands they wore. Orozco easily crushed the incompetently led government troops at the Battle of Rellano on March 25.[8]

To deal with Orozco, Madero was forced to call upon the Porfiriato army and to give command to the semiretired Brigadier General Victoriano Huerta to deal with Orozco. In April, Huerta proceeded north by train, bringing with him reinforcements that would increase the government's army to forty-eight hundred men. Pancho Villa, now commanding seven hundred irregular cavalrymen, joined Huerta at Torreón. The meeting harbored an omen for the future. Villa would write, "Huerta and his staff officers did not get up from their chairs that morning I walked into headquarters. I was dusty and tired. All the men there were dressed in gala uniforms. But because I was not in the regular army I was wearing my usual old clothes. I never forgot the way those men looked me up and down as if I were a stray mongrel that smelled bad."[9]

From mid-May through August, Huerta won a series of battles over Orozco, constantly pushing him north through the state of Chihuahua and driving him into the United States. Villa's irregular cavalry performed valuable service, but his lack of military decorum and refusal to take orders significantly irritated Huerta. The old-line general valued the spit-and-polish and discipline of the old army, all of which Villa ignored. Finally on June 4, in the middle of the campaign against Orozco, Huerta ordered Villa arrested for persistent insubordination. The event that climaxed Huerta's rage was Villa's refusal to return horses "confiscated" from a nearby ranch. Huerta ordered Villa to be shot the following morning.[10]

Few men have ever written about their experiences in front of a firing squad, but Villa is one.

> As I stood in the square the first sergeant of the platoon went up to the wall and made a cross on it. . . . The sergeant ordered me to stand at the foot of the mark. . . . I asked, . . . "Why are they going to shoot me?"
>
> I could not continue for the tears that choked me. At the time I hardly knew whether I was weeping from fear or mortification. . . .
>
> As the sergeant tried to force me to the wall I threw myself to the ground, pretending to beg but only fighting for time.[11]

Miraculously, fate intervened to save Villa. First, Colonel Rubio Navarrete convinced Huerta to temporarily stay the execution. In the meantime, Emilio and Raúl Madero had telegrammed their brother, the president, seeking a reprieve. This arrived shortly after Navarrete's intercession. Before being shipped off to prison in Mexico City, Villa presented Navarrete his horse and sword out of gratitude.[12]

While Huerta was completing the defeat of Orozco, the young Zapatista Gildardo Magaña was teaching Villa to read and write while in prison. Villa also learned of Zapata's goals, which centered on the return of communal lands (*ejidos*) from the large estates to the villages from which they had been stolen.[13]

On June 7, 1912, Villa was moved to the Santiago Tlatelolco Prison where General Reyes was being held. The general taught Villa civics and national history. Villa's confinement was not harsh. He was permitted to spend his own money to improve his furnishings, food, hygiene, and companionship. A young lady, Rosita Palacios, was a regular visitor.[14]

General Félix Díaz, nephew of Porfirio Díaz, was next to rebel. Following his uncle's downfall, Félix Díaz retired from the army and took up residence in Veracruz. Supported by some of the hierarchy of the Church, Díaz believed that he commanded wide support in his uncle's army, which was still intact. On October 16 Díaz seized Veracruz (285 miles east of Mexico City). Federal troops reacted rapidly and on October 23 a two-thousand-man force recaptured the port. Two days later, a local military court sentenced Félix Díaz to death. Friends interceded and Díaz was transferred to the Penitentiary of Mexico City where Madero commuted the death sentence.[15]

In the meantime, Pancho Villa languished in prison, his appeals going unanswered. He decided to escape and enlisted the help of a prison clerk, Carlos Jáuregui. A few days before his planned escape, a friend of General Bernardo Reyes, Antonio Tamayo, visited Villa, told him that there was a conspiracy to overthrow Madero, and invited him to join. Tamayo said, "Give us your word and in six days you will be free again."[16] Villa pretended to be interested but would have no part of a plot against Madero.[17]

On Christmas Day 1912, Pancho Villa and Carlos Jáuregui walked out the main gate of the prison. Villa made his way to Nogales, Sonora, and on January 2, 1913, crossed into Nogales, Arizona, as "Jesús José Martínez." He then traveled to El Paso, Texas, from where he sent word to Abraham González, a Maderista and the Governor of Chihuahua, concerning the plot against Madero. González passed this warning on to Madero but he ignored it as he did many others. González sent Villa some money and urged him not to return to Mexico for the time being.[18]

Mexico began 1913 filled with rumors of more uprisings. On Sunday, February 9, retired General Manuel Mondragón led several hundred soldiers to the Santiago Tlaltelolco Prison and freed General Bernardo Reyes. Others went to the Ciudadela (a barracks and arsenal) where Félix Díaz was being held and freed him. Simultaneously, the students of the Candidates' Military Academy, founded by General Reyes in Tlalpan, rebelled. They took streetcars to Mexico City. These rebels were also joined by other units as they approached the National Palace.[19]

In the meantime, General Lauro Villar, commander of the city's garrison, rose from his sick bed and rushed to the National Palace where Gustavo Madero had rallied soldiers loyal to his brother. An intensive fight broke out between the opposing sides. Within twenty minutes, eight hundred five bodies littered the plaza in front of the National Palace, most of them innocent civilians caught in the cross fire. Among the dead was General Reyes, killed by machine gun fire as he approached the National Palace on horseback. The rebels retreated to the Citadel, some twelve blocks from the National Palace. The armory housed 55,000 rifles, 30,000 carbines, 100 Hotchkiss machine guns, and 26 million 7-mm cartridges.[20]

Madero hurried from his residence in the Chapultepec Castle to the National Palace escorted by the cadets from the military academy; along the way the column was joined by General Huerta. Finding General Villar seriously wounded, Madero, acting on the insistence of his brother Gustavo, placed General Huerta in charge. Beginning on February 11, Huerta ordered infantry and cavalry attacks against the badly outnumbered rebels, all of which failed. Next, the two sides settled into an artillery duel with practically all of the shots falling among civilians. Only one shot hit the Citadel; two hit the National Palace. Both sides seemed intent on destroying the will of the populace to support Madero rather than hitting each other. The innocent dead were stacked like firewood, soaked in gasoline, and burned.[21]

Sickened by the loss of life, frustrated by the lack of progress, and perhaps suspicious of Huerta's intentions, Madero ordered General Felipe Angeles, who was directing operations against Zapata in the nearby state of Morelos, to return to the capital. The general returned with four hundred men and four machine

guns. However, Huerta, who was still in command, ordered Angeles to the suburbs to defend a possible (and virtually irrele-
vant) Zapatista attack.[22]

Beginning on Saturday, February 8, with the blessings of U.S.
Ambassador Henry Lane Wilson, the U.S. Embassy became the
meeting place for those opposed to Madero. In attendance were
American and Mexican businessmen and former leaders of the
Porfirio Díaz army. As the street fighting raged between Febru-
ary 9 and 18, these conspirators drew up the Pact of the Citadel
(*Pacto de la Ciudadela*).

On February 16 Ambassador Wilson invited Huerta, the
commander of Madero's forces, and the younger Díaz, the chief
rebel, to the embassy and urged them to unite against Madero.
Huerta needed no prodding. He ordered one of his protégés,
Brigadier General Aureliano Blanquet (who had been a member
of firing squad that shot Emperor Maximilian in 1867), to take
over the defense of the National Palace. Huerta then arrested the
president and vice president on February 18. On February 22 at
11:30 p.m., President Madero and Vice President José María Pino
Suárez were assassinated "while attempting to escape." Thousands, including many innocent civilians caught in the cross fire,
had died during the fighting of the "ten tragic days."[23]

Madero had made many military mistakes. He would not or
could not disband the irregular troops who had brought him to
power and thus became dependent upon the Porfiriato army to
deal with his former supporters, who demanded immediate
changes which he would or could not deliver. Neither the army
nor the irregulars were being regularly paid, thus undermining
their loyalty to the central government and, reinforcing their
loyalty to their officers and *caudillos*; their leaders provided for
their needs, frequently by extralegal means. Nonetheless,
Madero did not deserve his fate and needed to be avenged.[24]

Chapter 3

Fighting Huerta, 1913–14

T HE WEALTHY of the world were reassured by
Madero's "demise," whereas the humble were shocked by his
"murder." Most world powers recognized Huerta's government.
The Roman Catholic Church loaned him large sums and sang a
Te Deum in his honor; English banks floated him huge bonds.
On the other hand, the President of the United States, Woodrow
Wilson, and many Mexicans, including Pancho Villa, were hor-
rified by Madero's murder. President Wilson refused to recognize
Huerta's government and recalled Ambassador Henry Lane Wil-
son for his destructive meddling. Villa, still hiding in the United
States, possessed a burning desire to avenge Madero.[1]

Venustiano Carranza, governor of Coahuila and a supporter
of Madero, was one of three northern governors who refused to
recognize Huerta as the legal president of Mexico. At first glance,
it seemed that Carranza, governor of a poor, sparsely populated
state, stood little chance against the usurper who controlled the
resources of the central government. After all, Huerta had inher-
ited the Porfiriato army, which, in spite of its shortcomings, had

not been destroyed. The army numbered twenty-eight thousand men in April 1913.[2]

Revolutionary *caudillos* began to choose sides. Pascual Orozco chose Huerta. But almost all of the other important *caudillos*—Benjamín Hill, Alvaro Obregón, Pablo González, and Pancho Villa—chose Carranza. As he had in the past, Emiliano Zapata, existing in his own world, opposed Huerta but did not give allegiance to Carranza. Now Huerta, like Porfirio Díaz before him, became the glue that held these disparate revolutionaries together.[3]

In February 1913 Sonoran revolutionaries José María Maytorena and Adolfo de la Huerta (no relation to Victoriano Huerta) crossed the border and met with Pancho Villa in El Paso, Texas. They gave him $900 with which he bought a few weapons and supplies. On March 13, Villa and eight followers crossed back into Mexico riding stolen horses and trailing their meager supplies. Unfortunately for Villa, Huerta had had the governor of Chihuahua, Abraham González, assassinated on March 7. González had been one of the three northern governors opposed to Huerta. He was the individual who had commissioned Villa to recruit followers for the Madero uprising back in the fall of 1910. With his assassination, Villa lost the potential to acquire state funds and arms from the state arsenal. Once again Villa set out to raise a following, but this would take time.[4]

Typical of Villa's bravado, he sent the following telegram to his adversary, General Antonio Rábago: "Knowing that the government you represent was preparing to extradite me I have saved them the trouble."[5] Rábago countered with an offer of one hundred thousand pesos and the rank of general of division if Villa changed sides. Seldom at a loss for a retort, Villa replied, "Tell Huerta I do not need the rank as I am already supreme commander of free men that will achieve victory . . . and as for the 100,000 pesos, let him drink it up in *aguardiente* [a liquor derived from sugar cane]."[6]

While Villa was raising men and women and rustling cattle

from the huge estates belonging to the wealthy Terrazas family to buy guns and bullets, Venustiano Carranza, who, unlike Villa, Obregón, and González, was a politician and not a *caudillo*, sustained the only early defeat by the anti-Huerta revolutionaries. Carranza's followers took a severe beating at Saltillo (677 miles north-northwest of Mexico City) between March 21 and 23. To save himself, Carranza issued the Plan of Guadalupe on March 26, which was a call to arms against the usurper Huerta and a self-declaration naming himself the "First Chief" of the revolution. Next, Carranza fled west, skirting the territories controlled by the Huertistas while being careful not to enter the United States for fear of internment. By mid-September, he reached Hermosillo, capital of the Pacific Coast state of Sonora.[7]

While Carranza was slowly making his way to the safe but inaccessible capital of Sonora, Obregón was inflicting serious defeats on the Huertistas. In March and April, he captured the border towns of Nogales and Naco. Holding these two towns allowed him to export cattle to the United States and to import arms. After having won control of northern Sonora, Obregón turned south. He won battles at Santa Rosa (May 9–11, 1913) and Santa María (June 15–26), and besieged the port of Guaymas on June 27. He continually extended his operations south down the west coast.[8]

On July 4, Carranza reorganized the revolutionary army. He gave the most important commands to General Alvaro Obregón (the Northwestern Army Corps, which "on paper" included what would become known as the Division of the North commanded by General Francisco Villa) and General Pablo González (the Northeastern Army Corps), a good organizer but timorous fighter.

Below Mexico City, Zapata continued his hit-and-run tactics. Huerta responded with draconian measures; these increased the hostilities of the peons toward the government. But the government troops had little success in the countryside in spite of their brutal tactics. Zapata's nearness to Mexico City required Huerta to commit significant resources against him. However, Zapata's lack of arms and munitions prevented him from being a more potent threat.[9]

In the state of Chihuahua, Pancho Villa's irregular cavalry also went on the offense. On May 29, Villa captured Saucillo, Chihuahua, seizing much-needed arms. On June 19, seven hundred Villistas stormed Casas Grandes. After two hours of fighting, some four hundred *Colorados* fled; sixty were not fortunate enough to escape. Villa lined them up three deep and shot the *Colorados* in that alignment, each bullet passing through three men.[10]

Villa defeated small, isolated Huertista garrisons at San Andrés, Camargo, and Jiménez. On September 29, the lesser *caudillos* chose Villa to lead them and united into what became known as the Division of the North (*División del Norte)*. This placed Villa in command of about eight thousand followers.[11]

And what a gathering of individualists it was—Tomás Urbina, Maclovio Herrera, Calixto Contreras, Toribio Ortega, Agustín Castro, Eugenio Aguirre Benavides, and Manuel Chao. Urbina joined Villa with six hundred men and wagonloads of loot taken from Durango; unable to read or write, Urbina signed documents by drawing the shape of a heart. Herrera was a miner from Parral, and four hundred men and women followed him. In 1905 Contreras had protested against the excesses of the Porfirio Díaz government and was taken by force (*la leva*) into the army. Ortega was a cattleman from Chihuahua. He justly earned the sobriquet "The Honorable" because he did not execute prisoners and lived on his meager salary. Castro had been a streetcar conductor. The cross-eyed Eugenio Aguirre Benavides was a member of a prominent family and had been among the first to join the Madero movement. Chao had been the director of the school Nombre de Díos in Durango.[12]

In late September 1913, Pancho Villa continued to move south out of north-central Mexico straight for Torreón (446 miles north-northwest of Mexico City). Torreón was a new city that had recently sprung up for two reasons. First, it was the commercial center for the rapidly evolving cotton-growing industry, and second it was the key railroad junction for north central Mexico. Some three thousand individuals defended the city: two thousand Huertistas plus one thousand irregulars. These were *Colorados*, who knew their fate should Villa capture them, and Spaniards, who knew that Villa perceived them to be exploiters of the poor. Villa charged head on. Supported by only six home-made cannons and two machine guns, he possessed few alternatives other than a frontal assault. Fighting raged in the foothills for three days. By the evening of October 1, the Villistas had penetrated the outskirts of the city. That evening Villa ordered his troops to remove their hats so that they could identify each other and they burst into the city from three sides. Most of the outnumbered garrison escaped east behind the swollen Nazas River.[13]

The bounty was enormous—forty railroad engines and numerous cars; thirteen field pieces plus *El Niño* (a 3-inch railroad gun); six machine guns; six hundred grenades; one thousand rifles; and five hundred thousand cartridges. And there were fringe benefits; he acquired another new wife—Juanita Torres—after a whirlwind courtship.[14]

Both Villa's humanity and brutality exploded at Torreón. Appalled by the lack of care for his wounded, he ordered the creation of hospital trains. This was much more than just transportation for the sick and wounded. Cars were outfitted with operating rooms and other facilities. Eventually, sixty doctors—Mexicans and Americans—and a hundred nurses would service his hospital trains. Yet the same Villa turned his followers loose on the Chinese in Torreón. For if there were a nationality that Villa despised more than the Spaniards, it was the Chinese. This was a prejudice that Villa shared with many of the poor in northern Mexico. Some two hundred Chinese were slaughtered, many after being tortured.[15]

Villa also extracted a $300,000 peso "loan" from the banks of this city of twenty-six thousand inhabitants. After Villa departed Torreón, the bankers refused to pay the full amount. So, using one of his railway engines, he rushed back and as he wrote, "I reminded them that I was not playing games. The money belonged to the nation. . . . The people could take it when they needed it; and I could seize not only the amount of the loan but everything. . . . There was no more trouble."[16]

Back in Mexico City, Huerta was becoming increasingly dictatorial. On October 10, the Mexican senate demanded that senator Belisario Domínguez, who had severely criticized the Huerta government and then disappeared, be returned to that legislative body. Huerta, who could not raise the dead even if he wanted to, dissolved the Congress and imprisoned the remaining one hundred ten congressmen who opposed him.[17]

Meanwhile, Villa chose to leave only a small garrison in Torreón, appreciating that he was overextended; he moved to consolidate his hold over the north-central border region. He attacked Chihuahua City, garrisoned by 6,300 Huertistas, on November 5. The Division of the North overran the outer defenses but was then halted by the Huertista artillery. Although Villa had captured artillery at Torreón, making it serviceable with trained gun crews was another matter. Leaving some troops and his camp followers behind as a decoy, Villa seized two trains pulling coal cars at the Terrazas Station, north of Chihuahua City. He emptied the cars and loaded his troops on board. The trains then steamed north toward the border town Ciudad Juárez, two hundred miles away. At intervening stations, Villa telegraphed Ciudad Juárez requesting instructions, pretending to be the federal officer in charge of the trains and claiming that the rebels were blocking his way south. He was ordered to proceed to Ciudad Juárez. The trains loaded with Villistas rumbled into the border town uncontested during the night of November 15 and startled the garrison. After a brief fight with the surprised troops, Villa was victorious. General Hugh Scott, the local U.S. military commander, wrote, "He [Villa] captured [Ciudad] Juárez by a brilliant stroke of genius unlooked for from him, a coup of which any soldier would be proud."[18]

Not a single Villista was killed. Seventy-four Huertistas were executed, but not their commander, General Cesáreo Castro. He had been one of those officers who had convinced Huerta not to execute Villa back in June 1912. Castro was allowed to cross to El Paso, Texas. The capture of Ciudad Juárez was an important victory—with access to legal supplies and illegal weapons and munitions from the United States, Villa increased his independence from Carranza.[19]

Villa demonstrated his political astuteness by meeting with the mayor of El Paso and assuring him that he would protect American lives and fight the anticipated Huertista relief column far enough south that errant shells would not fall into the United States. Villa ordered Rodolfo Fierro to tear up the tracks leading to Ciudad Juárez. He destroyed the tracks forty-five miles south of Ciudad Juárez, forcing the Huertistas to disembark from their eleven trains and advance on foot.[20]

On November 21, Villa ordered a review of the division, ostensibly to celebrate the anniversary of Madero's call to arms but in reality to confuse the spies he knew to be present. Immediately following the parade, the six thousand three hundred troops boarded trains, steamed south for thirty-five miles, and disembarked at Tierra Blanca. The American soldier of fortune I. Thord-Gray described Villa's army:

> The troops moved in units, but in a Gypsy kind of formation. Only one regiment, Villa's own, and perhaps one more, marched in anything resembling military order. With but few exceptions, the rank and file did not wear uniforms, but carried their carbines and bandoleers over their shabby clothing with as much pride of bearing as members of any Imperial Guard.[21]

Villa held the high ground; the six thousand Huertistas were on a sandy, waterless plain. Throughout the twenty-second, the two sides waited for the other to make the first move. Villa grew impatient and planned to attack that night when his scouts told him that the Huertista cavalry was on the move, so he waited.[22]

The Huertistas attacked Villa's right flank in an unsuccessful attempt to capture the water towers at the Bauche railway station. The Huertistas' situation was growing more critical by the day because of their shortage of water. The Huertistas had only what they had carried with them from Chihuahua City, whereas the Villistas were modestly supplied from Ciudad Juárez. However, Villa also had problems; he had withheld no reserves, his battle line was dangerously overextended, and his troops had little ammunition. On November 24 the Huertistas attacked Villa's left flank but were beaten back again. The two Huertista flank attacks had forced Villa to extend his thin line farther. Desperate from lack of water, the Huertistas attacked along the entire front, and it appeared as if Villa's left flank might collapse. Then Villa threw all caution to the wind and ordered a massive cavalry change while one cavalry regiment from each flank circled behind the Huertistas. The Huertista infantry was caught in the open and the Huertista artillery was bogged down in the soft sand.[23]

During this assault, Rodolfo Fierro demonstrated his great value to Villa. In addition to being a cold-blooded assassin, he was recklessly brave and knowledgeable about railroads and dynamite. He led a raiding party that captured an inbound Huertista train. He packed it with dynamite and sent it speeding toward the enemy. It crashed into the parked Huertista trains causing great destruction. Toward the end of the battle, Fierro at full gallop overtook an escaping train, leaped on a car, climbed toward the engine, released the air from the brake cylinder, and brought the train to a halt. The Villistas fell on the train and slaughtered the escaping Huertistas.[24]

The Huertistas were first routed and then slaughtered in one of the bloodiest battles of the ten-year revolution. More than one thousand Huertistas died; the remainder escaped because Villa's horses had been weakened by a lack of food or water for almost two days. The booty was great—four locomotives and much rolling stock, eight field guns with ammunition, *El Niño* (a 3-inch railroad siege gun), seven machine guns, four hundred rifles, four hundred thousand rounds of ammunition, plus seventy thousand pesos.[25]

The defeat at Tierra Blanca sent shock waves through Chihuahua City. The Huertistas decided to evacuate the city and flee to Ojinaga. Three caravans left the provincial capital. The first was composed of sixteen wagons carrying 617 bars of silver belonging to the Alvarado Mining Company. The second caravan comprised the city's elite, including the affluent Terrazza family. The third caravan was made up of General Salvador Mercado's intact army: four hundred officers, five thousand men, twelve hundred women, and many children. Much of Mercado's army deserted before his eyes as he was forced to abandon the rail line at Falomir and to march through the desert. Meanwhile, anarchy reigned in Chihuahua City until December 8 when Pancho Villa entered the state capital and seized the governorship. He confiscated the property of the elites, especially the Terrazas family who were enemies of the revolution. This wealth was used to pension widows and orphans of fallen soldiers and to fund the State Bank of Chihuahua. In spite of his position of power, Villa did not make himself rich. He lowered the cost of basic necessities through rationing and controlled the distribution. He put his army to work fixing the city's damaged infrastructure—streets, telephone lines, water works—and in the slaughterhouses. The law was simple—violators were shot. Villa reasoned, "The only thing to do with soldiers in time of peace is to put them to work."[26]

Villa also took revenge on his enemies, and, by his definition, the enemies of the poor. He told the British vice-consul, Mr. Henry Scobell (who represented Spanish interests), "Any Spaniard caught within the boundaries of this state [Chihuahua] after five days will be escorted to the nearest wall by a firing squad."[27] Most of the Spaniards, leaving their possessions behind, escaped to Torreón, which had been reoccupied by the Huertistas.

Although the patriarch Luis Terrazas had escaped via Ojinaga to El Paso with twenty wagons of loot, the Villistas did capture his namesake and eldest son. The 52-year-old Luis had taken refuge in the British consulate in Chihuahua City, but the Villistas, not recognizing such an archaic concept as diplomatic sanctuary, dragged him out of his hiding place. The younger Luis was tortured to force him to reveal any hidden wealth. He was denied alcohol, a personal weakness, and hanged several times but each time rescued before dying. Luis finally revealed a hiding place containing $500,000. Eventually he escaped, but not before his health was broken. He died shortly thereafter in the United States.[28]

It was around this time that Pancho Villa created what became known as the *Dorados* (The Golden Ones) because of gold insignia on their olive-colored uniforms and Stetson hats. This handpicked force was organized into three squadrons of one hundred men each. Each man possessed two superb mounts and was armed with a rifle and two pistols. The *Dorados* were permitted no camp followers to slow them down.[29]

Villa sent General Pánfilo Natera and Toribio Ortega to capture Ojinaga from the five thousand Huertistas under Mercado who had abandoned Chihuahua City. Another border town, Ojinaga was one hundred fifty miles to the northeast of Chihuahua City and lay across the Rio Grande from Presidio, Texas. Natera and Ortega proved inept, so the impatient Villa decided to take matters in his own hands. Villa resigned his governorship and arrived on the outskirts of Ojinaga on January 9, 1914. On the tenth Villa attacked the Huertistas, and after a daylong battle during which both sides sustained heavy casualties, the Huertista army of five thousand men and women fled cross the Rio Grande into internment. Among those who escaped into the United States were Pascual Orozco and General Mercado. Villa had succeeded in one day where his subordinates had failed in four days of fighting.[30]

What might be considered flamboyant and even bizarre behavior to many was frequently the norm for Pancho Villa. On January 3, 1914, Villa's officers signed an exclusive contract with the Mutual Film Corporation to film their exploits. This could only have been done with Villa's knowledge and permission. In compensation, Villa's officers received twenty-five thousand dollars and the men got food and uniforms. Thousands of feet of footage were shot. Pancho, an excellent horseman, could not refrain from showing off; he would intentionally gallop full speed past the camera, constantly requiring the crew to plead with him to slow down. *The Life of General Villa* opened at the Lyric Theater in New York City on May 9, 1914.[31]

While the Huertista government was fighting in the north against Villa and other *caudillos*, Huerta attempted to transform Mexico into a military arsenal. Non-war-related businesses were forbidden to remain open on Sundays so that reservists could be trained, military cargos choked out all other railroad traffic, and technology and machinery necessary to manufacture munitions and weapons poured into Mexico. Huerta constantly decreed increases in the size of the army until it reached 250,000 men on paper on March 16, 1914, but these goals could not be realized by any means. Not even the *leva*, or forced conscription, could fill in the ranks. The officer corps expanded, and many advanced in grade rapidly, primarily as rewards for nonmilitary activities. By late 1913 the army had grown to its ultimate size, perhaps eighty thousand men, but the effectiveness of the Federal Army was being destroyed from within.[32]

These untrained, poorly led men frequently surrendered en masse. When they fought, they wasted ammunition at a prodigious rate. The Federal Army frequently expended more ammunition in a single battle than could be produced in Mexico during an entire month. Huerta ordered weapons and munitions from anyone who would sell to him, legally or illegally. Within this procurement system, graft and corruption grew to overwhelming proportions. It became in the financial interests of many of Huerta's supporters to prolong the fighting, not end it.[33]

Huerta chose to concentrate his raw and reluctant army in the cities, particularly those that possessed railroad junctions. This permitted his troops to fight from prepared defenses and made it very difficult to surprise them. However, the railroads were not a reliable source of supplies and reinforcements because the trains were easy prey for the fast-moving, hard-hitting cavalry of the rebels. The rebels always had the choice of the time and place of the battle.[34]

Regardless of how disruptive, these hit-and-run railroad raids were conducted by rifle-bearing irregulars. The rebels were too lightly armed to successfully attack towns defended by machine gun and artillery-equipped garrisons. The rebels needed to evolve into regular armies with artillery and machine guns and a well-thought-through strategy. In late 1913, American mercenary I. Thord-Gray observed the following concerning Villa's artillery: "A few minutes later he [Villa] proclaimed me as his 'Chief of Artillery' with the rank of first captain. My command consisted of two 75 mm field guns, no officers, no noncoms. There was a few half-wild Apache gunners who knew nothing about guns and some could not speak but their own language, except a little pigeon-Spanish."[35]

The creator of the strategy that would now be employed against the Huertistas was Felipe Angeles. Following Madero's assassination, Angeles, who had been temporarily imprisoned by Huerta, had been permitted to go to France. Huerta possibly refrained from assassinating Angeles because of his popularity among the recent graduates of the Chapultepec Military Academy. From France, Angeles traveled back to Mexico and joined Carranza. Angeles' strategy was to create regular armies out of the three major forces in the north and to have three revolutionary armies led by Obregón, González, and Villa drive south along each of the three major rail lines that ran from northern Mexico to the capital. The three armies would converge near Querétaro (100 miles northwest of Mexico City) where Carranza would take personal command and advance on the capital.[36]

In February 1914 the United States lifted the unevenly enforced arms embargo that it had imposed in 1912. Although this favored the rebels, it had little practical value since the anti-Huerta forces, thanks to Pancho Villa and Alvaro Obregón, controlled the border crossings and were already importing large amounts of contraband thinly disguised in crates marked "pianos" and the like.[37]

By now Carranza appreciated that while at Hermosillo he was isolated from the primary theater of fighting, the north central states. In February 1914 he began a trek to Chihuahua, once again being careful not to enter the United States. While en route, Carranza received a request from Pancho Villa for the services of General Felipe Angeles, to take charge of his artillery.

The union of Villa and Angeles changed the character of the Division of the North. Until now, in spite of its size, the division was simply a hard-hitting irregular cavalry. Angeles brought an understanding of military organization, strategy, tactics, and modern weapons—the machine gun and artillery piece. Why Carranza honored Villa's request for the services of Angeles is unclear. He had initially appointed Angeles as his secretary of war. But this did not sit well with Obregón, who would at least in theory be outranked by Angeles. Therefore, Carranza changed Angeles's position to sub-secretary of defense. Perhaps the reason why Carranza honored Villa's request was that he believed that Angeles, a man known for moral correctness, would be a thorn in the side of the murderous, hot-tempered Villa.[38]

Villa welcomed Angeles's arrival in Chihuahua City with a parade and an enthusiastic *abrazo* (embrace). Whomever Villa warmly embraced, those close to him quickly did as well. Although they had not previously met, Angeles had written to Villa congratulating him on his successes. These men of seemingly opposite personalities and virtues immediately became fast friends. Each man admired the other for his openness and his unique military skills. Also, both had elevated the dead Madero to a saintly status, giving them an additional bond.[39]

On the other hand, the relations between the impulsive Villa and the calculating Carranza deteriorated. Villa perceived the *Primer Jefe* to be coldly ambitious, while Carranza saw Villa as increasingly uncontrollable. On February 17 an incident occurred that caused Villa considerable international embarrassment and increased the strain between Villa and Carranza. William Benton, a hot-tempered Scotsman who had lived in northern Mexico for decades and had built up a highly successful ranch, went to see Villa about the excesses committed against his property by Villistas. Benton and Villa argued, and Villa ordered Rodolfo Fierro, his favorite assassin, to shoot Benton. Instead, Fierro bashed in his head with a shovel.

This created a maelstrom in the international press and among the world's powers. Execution by "shovel" was difficult to explain. Great Britain and France argued that the United States had a responsibility under the Monroe Doctrine to protect their citizens. Finally, Carranza took Villa off the "political" hook by requiring all inquiries to be addressed to Carranza as the "First Chief" of the revolution. The incident caused considerable international embarrassment.[40]

Next, the issuing of money became the cause of conflict between Villa and Carranza. Villa requested from Carranza five million pesos to finance his next offensive against Torreón. Carranza responded that he could not provide that amount. Villa then set up presses in the basement of the governor's palace in Chihuahua City and printed two million pesos. Carranza sent the lawyer Luis Cabrera to reign Villa in. All he was able to get was a promise that Villa would not print any more than was absolutely necessary.[41]

In March Carranza finally arrived in Chihuahua City and met Villa face to face, and it was not love at first sight. Not only were their personalities opposite, but the attributes that each possessed were those that the other loathed. Villa possessed a streak of wildness that could be destructive or creative. Carranza had a vein of cunning that could be devious or constructive. Villa later commented, "I embraced him energetically, but with the first words we spoke my blood turned to ice. I saw that I could not open my heart to him. As far as he was concerned, I was a rival, not a friend. He never looked me in the eye. . . . There was nothing in common between that man and me."[42] The atmosphere in Chihuahua City was uneasy while the politician who commanded the revolution, Carranza, shared the state capital with the *caudillo* who controlled the state, Villa.

Pancho Villa planned to march south and attack Torreón; the city was the key to advancing into central Mexico. It was the strategic railroad junction where the principal line from Mexico City divided. One branch ran north-northwest through Chihuahua City to the American border before the branch, splitting in two, ran east to Monterrey and then ultimately to the American frontier. Villa's irregular cavalry had previously captured Torreón in October 1913, but he had left only a small guard, using most of his forces to secure his base of support in the north. In the meantime, Huertista Gen. José Refugio Velasco had recaptured the city. While Villa was capturing Ciudad Juárez, Chihuahua, and Ojinaga, Velasco was fortifying Torreón with artillery, machine guns, barbed wire, and trenches. He boasted that Torreón was impregnable.[43]

Villa shrouded his intentions by cutting all communications between Chihuahua and Torreón. He cut rail, road, and telegraph lines and used cavalry to patrol the countryside. On March 16 Villa's sixteen-thousand-man Division of the North, which Angeles had organized into companies, brigades, and regiments, began moving south by train. Villa designated Angeles as chief of artillery and his successor should he be disabled.[44]

The first trains were loaded with cavalry. The horses rode inside the boxcars while the men rode on top. Next came two construction trains to repair any damaged rail. Then came two artillery trains. The artillery had been organized into two regiments of four batteries each. Most of the guns were of French manufacture and were 70 mm, 75 mm, and 80 mm in size. Plus, there were two large railroad guns. Then came a hospital train equipped for surgery. Finally, there was a headquarters train that, among other items, possessed a press car and carriages carrying machine gun units and reserve ammunition. Finally, there were the troop trains, carrying an army that more closely resembled a collection of migrants. On March 17, some seventy miles north of Torreón, the Villistas off-loaded their trains. There they waited for three days while Villa attended a wedding—this time not one of his own.[45]

On March 20, the Villistas continued south, paralleling the tracks with their trains slowly following. The northernmost Huertista outpost was at Bermejillo, twenty-seven miles outside of Torreón. It was defended by the Orozquista General Benjamín Argumedo, commanding both *Colorados* and federal soldiers. Argumedo, seeing dust to the north, sent out scouts who were soon captured by Villa. The Villistas surprised the defenders at Bermejillo and they subsequently fled, departing so fast that they left the phone line to Torreón Huertistas intact. So Angeles talked to Velasco, whom he knew well, and unsuccessfully tried to convince him to surrender.[46]

The Villistas continued to march down the tracks. They defeated Huertista outposts at Mapimí and Tlahualillo. At Noé, eight miles north of Torreón, the Villistas found the tracks torn up. While repairing them, Villa sent troops to block the various avenues of escape from Torreón.[47]

On March 22 Villa, commanding the center, ordered a general attack against Gómez Palacio, a sister city to Torreón sitting on the Río Nazas four miles to the west. Streetcars connected the two cities. Villa, tied down by the fighting in the center, was unable to give overall directions. As a result, the attackers dissipated their energies, and the assault bogged down. In addition, the artillery ammunition that the rebels had manufactured in Chihuahua City proved to be, for the most part, duds. Villista casualties mounted; these included men who died from drinking water from the irrigation ditches that the Huertistas had poisoned. The only thing that prevented a disaster was the reluctance of the Huertistas to move out of their well-prepared defenses and attack.[48]

After a brief respite, Villa renewed the assault, and for three days he threw men against the entrenched Huertistas. Angeles wanted to move his artillery closer to compensate for the poor-quality powder in his shells. However, the Huertista artillery was mounted on a hill, La Pila, to the west of Gómez Palacio, and dominated the battlefield. Consequently, the Villistas quickly relaid the torn-up tracks and brought up their two large railroad guns. Once darkness fell, Angeles moved his field pieces forward, and together the Villista artillery concentrated on the hill. During the night of March 25, Villistas led by Herreras, Urbina, and Rodríguez captured La Pila in fierce fighting, taking the machine gun and artillery emplacements in hand-to-hand fighting.[49]

The next morning Huertistas from Torreón counterattacked. They swept over the hill and charged the Villista artillery, which was less than one mile from the base of La Pila. Angeles stemmed the panic among his artillerymen and they turned back to attack. Villa ordered another assault on the hill for that night; however, the Huertistas were content to withdraw their artillery and Villa found the hill deserted. The Villistas entered the abandoned Gómez Palacio on the twenty-sixth.[50]

Villa then asked the British vice-consul in Gómez Palacio, Herbert Cummins, to convey surrender terms to General Velasco. Should the Huertistas surrender, Villa would spare the lives of the men and the officers as well. At first Cummins declined to carry the message. After some harsh words between the two men, both reconsidered their positions. Villa apologized for his threatening manner, and Cummins decided to deliver the message. Velasco refused the offer.[51]

Villa's men then fought their way into Torreón. Block by block, the fighting ebbed and flowed under savage attacks and equally savage counterattacks. On April 1 the Villistas tenaciously fought their way into the center of the city only to be pushed out again. The American consul in Torreón, George C. Carothers, proposed to Villa that the Huertistas be permitted to withdraw. Villa would have none of that—either he surrendered or he fought to the death.[52]

At midday on April 2, the Huertista artillery began a heavy barrage on the Villista positions to the north and west of Torreón. Villa, anticipating a ground attack, moved troops from the east. Velasco, under the fortuitous cover of a dust storm, escaped east. His trains, covered by the *Colorado* cavalry, streamed unmolested out of Torreón toward Saltillo.

Notwithstanding Velasco's escape, the capture of Torreón was a major victory for Villa. He captured thousands of European-manufactured artillery shells and a million rounds of small arms ammunition. He also took one hundred thousand bales of cotton and rail yards full of locomotives and railroad cars.[53]

Also, Villa once again administered justice to some seven hundred Spaniards, many of whom he had driven out of Chihuahua City a few months earlier. Villa confiscated their property, loaded them into railroad cars, and transported them with little food or water across five hundred miles of mostly desert to the American border.[54]

Villa's military status grew from that of a talented guerrilla to a victorious field general. The decisive advantage held by the Villistas at Torreón was their greater willingness to die for their cause in comparison with the Huertistas. Rafael Muñoz described the fighting spirit of the Villistas: "They surrounded the cities no matter how large they were; they flooded the cities no matter how sprawling. They would move launching shouts of enthusiasm amid the streams of blood. They fell seeing others advance. Before clouding over forever, their eyes would be dazzled with victory."[55]

In spite of the fact that Villa's only strategy was frontal assaults against an entrenched enemy, the Villistas had won.[56]

While the battle of Torreón raged, Carranza appointed General, Manuel Chao, a subordinate of Villa, as the military governor of the state of Chihuahua. This was an oblivious attempt to limit Villa's growing independence. Villa was furious. He ordered Chao to report for duty at Torreón. Chao, after consulting with Carranza, refused. Villa ordered Chao seized and shot. Carranza interceded and had Chao released; grudgingly, Villa acceded.[57]

The six thousand Huertistas had escaped from Torreón to the east, and even though the road to Mexico City appeared open, Villa did not believe that he could march south with Velasco's army to his rear. Velasco reached Viesca, forty-five miles to the east of Torreón, where he found the tracks had been torn up. In

the meantime, a six-thousand-man Huertista relief force commanded by General Joaquín Maass arrived at San Pedro de las
Colonias, forty-five miles north of Viesca. Villa sent troops to
eliminate these Huertista forces. On April 4 the Villistas attacked both Viesca and San Pedro. General Velasco, almost out
of ammunition, broke through the attackers and joined Maass at
San Pedro.[58]

The successful union of the Huertista forces angered Villa so
much he took personal command of the attack. On April 12, the
Villista artillery opened a devastating fire on the poorly entrenched Huertistas. On the fourteenth Villa launched an all-out
assault against San Pedro. The Huertistas gave no ground. But
Velasco and Maass, both "generals of division," argued over
command. Velasco deserted Maass to his own resources on the
fifteenth and withdrew east. Once again, Argumeda's *Colorados*
covered his retreat. Next, Maass abandoned San Pedro and retreated toward Saltillo while under constant attack from the Villistas. Both sides sustained heavy casualties. As Velasco and
Maass continued their retreats toward Saltillo their armies disintegrated—men deserted en masse.[59]

Villa's victory at Torreón and San Pedro made him the *max-
imo caudillo* of the north. Now he virtually ignored Carranza,
who was still in Chihuahua City. Villa issued his own currency,
confiscated property, crops, livestock, and ores to pay for the
needs of his army. He sent procurement agents to El Paso, Texas,
to buy weapons and munitions.[60]

In the fighting at Torreón, Viesca, and San Pedro, Villa had
sustained some five thousand casualties. But Huerta had lost
about eight thousand men, and two of his armies, those commanded by Velasco and Maass, ceased to exist. Villa now returned to Chihuahua City to prepare for future campaigns and
to protect his base of support, not from Huerta but from Carranza. Fortunately for Carranza, his other generals were winning
battles, thus stealing some of Villa's glory. Pablo Gonzalez, leading the Northeast Army Corps, defeated the Huertistas in the
states of Coahuila, Nuevo León, and Tamaulipas. On April 24

Gonzalez occupied Monterrey, the most important industrial city of the north.[61]

While Villa and others were taking control of the north, the United States seized Veracruz on April 21, 1914, on the pretext that the Huerta government had (which the United States did not recognize) refused to properly apologize and salute the American flag following an incident at Tampico earlier in the month. In part, the United States wanted to block the delivery of seventeen million rounds of ammunition being carried in the German merchant ship *Ypiranga*. The American plan misfired. The *Ypiranga* was warned of the American trap and diverted to Tampico where it successfully delivered its cargo to the Huertistas. Although the Huertistas guarding Veracruz were intimidated by the U.S. Marines and chose to flee without a fight, not so for the naval academy cadets and infuriated civilians. Armed with antiquated weapons, they fought a losing battle throughout the day. The Mexicans lost 193 dead; 600 were wounded. The Americans lost 19 dead and had 70 wounded.[62]

The American action won Huerta sympathy among some Mexicans who now perceived the United States as a bigger threat than the continuation of the Huerta government. The United States gratefully accepted the proffered mediation of Argentina, Brazil, and Chile in an attempt to escape the increasingly embarrassing occupation.[63]

Elsewhere, rebel successes against Huerta continued. On May 14 Tampico, with its rich oil fields, fell to the Carrancista army led by Pablo González. Obregón fought south through the western states of Sinaloa and Nayarit. On May 16, 1914, he captured Tepic. Next, he invaded the state of Jalisco.[64]

The rebel campaign now took on the character of a race to Mexico City between the Villistas and the Carrancistas (the armies commanded by Obregón and González). Villa returned to Torreón. He planned to use the rail center as his staging point for the push toward Mexico City. Without consulting Carranza, Villa decided to attack Zacatecas. This would place him closer to Mexico City than either Obregón or Gonzalez. But Carranza had followed Villa to Torreón and interjected himself into the meetings concerning future campaigns. There, Carranza ordered Villa to attack Saltillo, 175 miles to the east, arguing that this was essential to secure Villa's left flank. Carranza chose to ignore the fact that González' army was in Monterrey a mere fifty miles east of Saltillo.

Carranza, having successfully diverted Villa to Saltillo, traveled to Durango and met with General Pánfilo Natera. When Natera told Carranza that with some reinforcements he could capture Zacatecas, Carranza entrusted him with the task.[65]

On May 11 Villa's trains began rolling out of Torreón toward Saltillo. They were loaded with cavalry, infantry, artillery, munitions, water, supplies, and extra railroad ties. The force stopped at San Pedro de las Colonias to take on some recently purchased mules from Kentucky; these would be needed to pull the field artillery. The bulk of the Villistas off-loaded at Estacion Sauceda.

The Huertistas positioned themselves to block whichever east-west rail line the enemy might take. There were five thousand Huertistas under General Maass at Saltillo; two thousand under Orozco at Ramos Arizpe; and five thousand under various generals at Paredón. These three forces could readily unite using the north-south railroad that ran through Saltillo and Paredón. Angeles recommended to Villa that a two-thousand-man force be sent to cut the north-south rail line at Estación Zertuche, while the main body attack the Huertistas at Paredón. Villa agreed with the strategy.

On May 17 Villa's forces were in position. Villa and Angeles conferred, and Villa, sensing that the enemy was demoralized, told Angeles that he didn't think he would need Angeles's artillery. At ten o'clock, six thousand Villista cavalrymen charged. The poor Huertista defenses almost immediately collapsed; Angeles's guns did not fire a single shot. The Huertistas lost one thousand dead and two thousand captured. The remainder, mostly cavalry, escaped. Villa wrote, "Some of my men had the pleasure of bringing in fifteen or twenty prisoners each."[66] Felipe

Angeles interceded with Villa, saving two thousand Huertista soldiers from execution.[67]

But not all escaped the wrath of Villa. His soldiers brought two Huertista officers to Villa while he was eating lunch and asked what to do with them. Without hesitating, Villa said shoot them. Jesús Acuña, Carranza's onsite representative, objected. Villa shouted, "Why are you afraid to see the laws of the Revolution carried out? You chocolate drinking politicians want to triumph without remembering the blood-drenched battlefields."[68] The two officers were shot on the spot, and their bodies lay there until the meal was over. Villa entered Saltillo unopposed on the twenty-first and within a week turned it over to Gonzalez.[69]

Unfortunately for Carranza, he had underestimated Villa's military talents and overestimated those of Natera. While Villa was speedily capturing Saltillo, notwithstanding his taking time for affairs of the heart, Natera, commanding six thousand men and little artillery, was failing in his attacks against the ten thousand well fortified Huertistas in Zacatecas. Villa immediately returned to Torreón and prepared to move south.

On June 12 Carranza ordered Villa to detach five thousand troops and artillery under General José Isabel Robles from *El División del Norte* to reinforce General Natera's forces confronting Zacatecas.

This would significantly reduce Villa's command and weaken him militarily and politically. Villa replied that Robles was ill and could not immediately lead his troops south. Carranza then ordered that the troops be sent under the command of someone else. In Villa's defense, this was easy to say but difficult to achieve. Villa's army, like those of all *caudillos,* was feudal in nature. The men held a personal loyalty to their specific commander, who provided for their needs. Therefore suggesting that Robles' fighters be commanded by someone else was impractical. Obviously, adequate room for compromise existed, but neither Carranza nor Villa was interested in doing so.[70]

The showdown between Villa and Carranza came on June 13

as each dictated telegraphs to be sent to the other, Carranza in Saltillo and Villa in Torreón. They argued back and forth over the wires. Villa told Carranza that Robles was ill and could not lead the troops to Natera's relief. Carranza argued that someone else could command the men and insisted that they be sent. Villa, declaring that it was "just sending men to the slaughter-house," was enraged, and he resigned; Carranza almost immediately accepted, "with regret." Villa's generals were angry and despondent. Gen. Maclovio Herrera put a gun to the head of the telegraph operator and told him to send the following message: "Señor Carranza, I am informed of your treatment of my General Francisco Villa. You are a son of a bitch."[71]

As Herrera and Villa's other *caudillos* were spinning out of control, Felipe Angeles entered the railway station and restored order. The following day after cooling down, the generals of the Division of the North began exchanging telegrams with Carranza. Carranza refused to reinstate Villa and ordered the generals to choose a new chief. On June 15 the generals of the Division of the North telegraphed Carranza:

> Señor, from your last message we consider that you have not under-stood us or wished to understand. . . . We know well that you were looking for the opportunity to stop General Villa. . . . Before the interests and ambitions of the Chief come the sorrows and needs of the Mexican people . . . and the people tell us that General Villa must not give up his command. . . .[72]

Immediately, eleven of Villa's generals resigned from Carranza's Constitutional Army and prevailed upon Villa to continue to lead them. Theoretically, this made Villa independent of Carranza.

On June 17 the entire Division of the North, some 21,000 men and women, began moving toward Zacatecas without Carranza's authorization. Carranza notified his other military commanders of Villa's insubordination and that of the other generals in the Division. Obregón, González, and others sent telegrams reaffirming their loyalty to Carranza.[73]

Zacatecas lay on the principal rail line between Torreón and Mexico City. A city of thirty thousand inhabitants, it was here that Huerta had massed twelve thousand men commanded by Gen. Medina Barrón with orders to keep the northern hordes from penetrating into central Mexico at all costs. The Division of the North disembarked from its trains at Calera about fourteen miles north of Zacatecas. On the twenth the division reached Vetagrande, a small village on the heights above Zacatecas. From this position, Villa could see the enemy's defenses. Two heavily fortified ridges lay between the division and Zacatecas, and the rainy season had begun.[74]

Villa launched his attack on June 23. At ten o'clock, Villa's artillery opened fire; twenty minutes later, the infantry moved forward. As a hill was captured, the Villista artillery would be dragged forward. Villa personally commanded the right of his line against Benjamín Argumedo, an Orozquista. The Villistas captured the surrounding hills and closed most of the avenues of escape. The Huertistas found their position in Zacatecas indefensible. On the twenty-third they endeavored to flee. At this point, Felipe Angeles told his men, "Have no fear, they are not fighting, they are already fleeing, it is more a question of exterminating them."[75] Only two thousand Huertistas did escape, including the Orozquista Argumedo, toward Aguascalientes. The Huertistas lost five thousand killed, and many were captured. Villa lost five hundred killed, and fifteen hundred were wounded; his victory was decisive.[76]

Once again, Villa clashed with a local British representative. Villa accused the British vice-consul in Zacatecas, Donald St. Clair Douglas, of helping the Huertistas during the battle. Typically, summary execution was the fate of those so charged. However, Villa ordered a trial that was attended by the American vice-consul in Durango, Theodore C. Hamm. Douglas was acquitted but ordered to leave the country immediately.[77]

The road to Mexico City appeared open; no significant Huertista force remained to block Villa. However, the weight of the personnel and materiel losses upon Villa's Division at Tor-reón, San Pedro, and now Zacatecas had ground his army to a halt. Moreover, Carranza had stopped supplying Villa with coal for his trains and munitions for his guns. Villa needed to return north to gather more men and resources.[78]

At this time he held out an "olive branch" to Carranza. Villa sent a long, polite telegram detailing the battle for Zacatecas. Carranza was in no mood to "kiss and make up" and had already decided to inhibit Villa's movement south by cutting off all sup-plies. Although Villa had gained significant independence by controlling ports of entry from the United States, these could not supply all his needs. The most critical resource that Carranza controlled was coal, for without it, Villa's trains could not move. By now Obregón was nearing Guadalajara (424 miles west-northwest of Mexico City).[79]

Many among the rebels wanted reconciliation between Villa and Carranza. Although it appeared that Huerta's defeat was just a matter of time, an unreconciled Villa and Carranza cast a dark shadow over the future of Mexico. A forum for a compromise between the opposing camps offered itself in late June when Pablo González, commanding the Northeast Army Corps, sug-gested to Villa that they each send a commission to Torreón to discuss reconciliation between Villa and Carranza. Villa at-tempted to expand the meeting by inviting Orbegón, but he de-clined to attend.[80]

Interestingly, in an interview between Carranza and some agents of the U.S. Government held on July 1, Carranza stated that this meeting between Villa's and González' representatives was taking place at the initiative of the generals and he had not sent anyone. Given González's cautious nature, it is highly un-likely that he would initiate such a meeting without Carranza's approval.[81]

For his part, Villa was also exploring all options. On July 6, while the conference was taking place, Villa telegrammed Gen-eral Hugh Scott, commander of the Southern Department of the U.S. Army, asking what the American attitude would be toward a complete rupture between him and Carranza. Scott's reply was polite and noncommittal.[82]

By July 8 the six men, representing the two sides, struck a deal, at least on paper. The following were its most important terms. No member of the rebel armies or provisional official would seek permanent political office. Carranza would remain the "First Chief" and Villa would retain command of the Division of the North. Villa would be promoted to general of division, the rank held by Obregón and González. Villa would report to Carranza for "rectifications and ratifications." Carranza would provide Villa with coal and munitions and give him freedom of action in his area of domain. The coalfields at Muzquitz would be transferred to Villa's control. A Villista would remain in charge of the railroads in the north. Villa would release forty prisoners whom he held against Carranza's wishes. Villa would redeem paper money that he issued without Carranza's authority. The two sides agreed to a list of names from which Carranza, as interim president, would choose his cabinet. The meeting set the ground rules for the calling of a revolutionary convention. Land reform and social legislation were also promised.[83]

For Carranza, this pact conceded too much to Villa. He rejected almost all of the provisions agreed to by the representatives but never informed Villa, except through his actions. Carranza argued that these six men had exceeded any authority they might have had. The only positive result was that formal contact between Carranza and Villa was restored, but even this was fleeting.[84]

The weight of the Huertista losses in the north caused principally by Villa and Obregón, the constant pressure exerted by Zapata in the south, and to a lesser extent the American capture of Veracruz finally caused the collapse of the Huerta government. Huerta resigned on July 15, 1914. His defeat also marked the end of the federal army. On August 13 federal General Gustavo A. Salas signed the Treaties of Teoloyucán on the fender of an automobile. This required the disbanding of the federal army. Mex-

ico's traditional power brokers—the army, the landed aristoc-
racy, the business magnates, and the church—were irretrievably
damaged by Huerta's defeat.[85]

The educated, refined José Vasconcelos, who would not gain
an appreciation of the uneducated, barbarous Pancho Villa until
after his defeat, wrote: "There can be no doubt that Villa had
been the destroyer of the armies of the Huerta government. And
in that moment, without the Division of the North, neither
those [troops] of Obregón in Sinaloa, much less those of Don
Pablo [González] never would have arrived in the capital."[86]

Now the fight was between Villa and Carranza.

Chapter 4

Fighting Carranza, 1914–16

WHILE THE HUERTA GOVERNMENT was dis-
integrating, Obregón was winning the race to Mexico City—
Carranza had successfully delayed Villa's advance, temporarily
stranding his train-bound army in Zacatecas (325 miles northwest of Mexico City). Obregón entered Mexico City on August
15, 1914.[1]

Villa, undoubtedly appreciating by mid-July that he could
not win the race, returned to the north and began building his
forces for the inevitable fight with Carranza. Villa gathered up all
the men, cattle, and horses he could seize. The men he made
into soldiers, the cattle he sold to the United States for currency,
and the horses he used to create his cavalry. Although the United
States had declared an arms embargo against Mexico, it made
virtually no effort to enforce it.[2]

In late August, shooting erupted between revolutionary factions in the state of Sonora. Sonora was the political backyard of
Alvaro Obregón. Villa, who was endeavoring to extend his in-
fluence over the entire north, inserted himself in the squabble.
At issue was who would control the state—the governor, José

Maytorena, whom Villa supported, or the local military commander, Plutarco Calles, whom Obregón supported. Maytorena had Calles under siege in the border town of Naco. Villa and Obregón met with Maytorena at Nogales on August 29 and agreed that Maytorena should continue as governor but that the state would militarily remain under Obregón's control. However, so many of the revolutionary chiefs in Sonora objected that Villa and Obregón met again the following day, this time deciding that Obregón was to have total control but that Calles's troops would be turned over to Benjamín Hill and would remain in Naco. Villa and Obregón traveled to Chihuahua City, but there they learned that many revolutionaries even opposed this second agreement. A third agreement was therefore struck; Villa deferred to Obregón's solution. Juan Cabral was to be made governor of Sonora and the troops under Calles were to withdraw temporarily from the state.[3]

Now Villa and Obregón turned to national issues. Perhaps in earnest, Villa said to Obregón, "The destiny of the *Patria* [fatherland] is in your hands and mine; if we untie *in less than a minute* we'll tame the country, and, since I am a humble man, you'll be the President."[4] Obregón, possibly believing that Villa would or could not deliver on the proposal, did not respond.[5]

On September 3, Villa and Obregón signed a nine-point proposal. The most controversial point was that Carranza had to choose between being "the First Chief" and the opportunity to run as constitutional president. (This stipulation had also been part of the Pact of Torreón.) On September 9 Obregón returned to Mexico City and presented the document to Carranza. He rejected it using the same rationale he had when he rejected the "Pact" of Torreón—no handful of men should decide the fate of Mexico. Carranza, an astute politician, appreciated the need to improve the legitimacy of his position. He proposed to call together a junta of the revolutionary chiefs in the capital to offer him advice. Villa and other opponents wanted a convention that would dictate solutions.[6]

The relationship between Villa and Carranza was a tinderbox

of hate and mistrust awaiting a spark to ignite it. Renewed feuding in Sonora between José Maytorena and Benjamín Hill, hardly of national concern, proved to be that spark. Villa ordered Hill to withdraw from Sonora but he refused. In fact, Hill fell under Obregón's command rather than Villa's. Once again, Obregón traveled to Chihuahua in an attempt to defuse the issue. Few accounts of what transpired over the next few days agree.

Villa used a military parade on September 16, Independence Day, to try to impress Obregón with his strength. Fifty-two hundred men and forty-three pieces of artillery rumbled down the streets of Chihuahua past city hall. On the morning of the seventeenth, Villa told Obregón that Hill must withdraw; Obregón sent the order. However, Hill again refused arguing that Obregón was under duress. Apparently losing his temper, Villa shouted, "General Hill thinks that I can be played with. . . . You're a traitor and I'm going to have you executed right now."[7] Speaking calmly, Obregón stated that dying for the revolution would increase his stature. This startled Villa, and he broke into tears, saying, "Francisco Villa is not a traitor; Francisco Villa does not kill defenseless men, and certainly not you, my good friend, who are my guest."[8]

Villa and Obregón hammered out another agreement. It basically stated that a convention to include all revolutionary factions was needed and that Carranza's suggested "junta" was inadequate. The agreement called for a convention; the agenda was to include the discussion of political, social, and economic problems. At least on paper, it seemed that Obregón was in complete agreement with Villa and had professed that he also saw Carranza as the problem. Perhaps Obregón was so agreeable in order to facilitate his escape from Villa's clutches.[9]

Back in Mexico City, Carranza, hearing only disturbing rumors out of Chihuahua, feared that Obregón was a prisoner, or dead, and that Villa was on the march to the capital. Carranza ordered Pánfilo Natera to tear up the railroad tracks north of Zacatecas to inhibit Villa's advance. Natera, having no intelligence that Villa was on the move, hesitated. Later, Carranza would rescind the order once he possessed more accurate intelligence.[10]

Villa permitted Obregón to leave on the night of September 21. The train was hours down the tracks when Villa learned that Carranza had ordered the tracks leading to Chihuahua City torn up. Villa telegrammed Carranza that this was a hostile act and demanded an explanation. Carranza responded by demanding to know Obregón's fate. Villa retorted that Obregón had already departed for Mexico City. But now Villa, who controlled the railroad north of Torreón, ordered that Obregón be returned to Chihuahua City. The climax came as Villa withdrew his recognition of Carranza as the First Chief and stated he would not send a representative to the junta meeting.[11]

Obregón was intercepted north of Torreón and turned around; not even he knew what awaited him back in Chihuahua City. Again the two titans met face to face and hurled insults at each other. Villa accused Obregón of being a Carrancista, and Obregón retorted with the same accusation. He reminded Villa that he too had signed the Plan of Guadalupe that pledged him to Carranza's side. Obregón's boldness may well have saved his life—Villa loathed evasiveness.[12]

Villa permitted Obregón to leave once again. Prior to the departure of Obregón's train, another train carrying a small command under General Mateo Almanza left the station. He had orders from Villa to stop Obregón's train and execute the general. If Almanza truly had been ordered to kill Obregón, he missed his opportunity while on a sidetrack. Next, Obregón's train was to be stopped farther down the line so that Almanza could catch up. However, apparently friends diverted this message long enough for Obregón to escape. Obregón's survival was no less miraculous than that of Daniel in the lion's den.[13]

As far as Villa was concerned, the time for words had ended and the time had come for the lesser *caudillos* to choose sides. Villa was surprised that Maclovio Herrera withheld his support as did the brothers Domingo and Mariano Arrieta, who controlled much of the state of Durango. On September 30 Villa's army started moving south by train. The troops rumbled through Torreón and finally disembarked at Zacatecas.[14]

Meanwhile on October 1, Carranza called a meeting of those whom he perceived supported him, for there were no certainties in revolutionary Mexico. He was hoping to sell this gathering as a broad-based assembly of revolutionaries. But the absence of Villistas and Zapatistas would not permit the creation of this illusion. Moreover, those invited were not as submissive to Carranza as he had hoped.[15]

Elsewhere, other revolutionary leaders feverishly worked to head off a fight between Villa and Carranza. Finally, these leaders, who represented all factions except Zapatistas (who were later included), agreed to hold a convention in Aguascalientes (250 miles northwest of Mexico City). This was not what Carranza had wanted.[16]

By late 1914, Mexico was dissolving into armed camps: Venustiano Carranza, a pragmatist to some and an opportunist to others; Emiliano Zapata, the semirecluse champion of agrarian reform; and Pancho Villa, sometimes-bandit, sometimes-patriot; these three men towered above all others and were unsatisfied with the status quo. All the while, lesser *caudillos* waited to see who might be the strongest before choosing sides. Zapata controlled the south, Villa held the central north, and Carranza controlled the two coasts north of Mexico City and the northeast. The three revolutionary chiefs each sent representatives to Washington knowing that President Wilson could decide their fate should he choose to manipulate the flow of arms across the border.[17]

The opening of the gathering at Aguascalientes on October 10 proved a good omen for Pancho Villa because the convention declared itself a sovereign body. An overwhelming number of delegates were military men; they excluded those who had joined the fight late against Huerta. Eligibility was based on one delegate for each one thousand soldiers. One hundred and fifty-two delegates were initially seated. Villa set up headquarters at Guadalupe, one hundred miles north of Aguascalientes, and paid a brief visit to the convention. Meanwhile, all awaited the arrival of the Zapatistas. In many respects, this was like awaiting the entrance of a foreign delegation—few at the gathering knew southern Mexico, and by October 1914 Zapata had already become more of a legend than a man.[18]

Finally, the convention realized that the Zapatistas were inhibited from attending by their continuing opposition to Carranza. The First Chief controlled Mexico City through which the rail line passed on its way to Aguascalientes and beyond. Finally, the convention sent General Felipe Angeles and two others to personally invite Zapata and his delegation to attend. Angeles and Zapata met in Cuernavaca toward the end of October. Zapata agreed to send a twenty-six-man delegation as an interim representation. Those at the convention received the good news that the train carrying the Zapatistas passed through Mexico City uninhibited. On October 24 the train steamed into Aguascalientes and, to everyone's surprise, through the city without stopping. Its destination was Guadalupe where the *Zapatistas* first wanted to confer privately with Villa.[19]

Finally, on October 26 the twenty-six Zapatistas entered the Morelos Theater where the convention was being held. The remaining delegates outnumbered the Zapatistas and the thirty-seven Villistas. The following day, Zapatistas addressed the convention; some of the orations shocked the moderates present for the speakers included anarchists. Before long, the Zapatistas were lobbing verbal hand grenades into the assembly. They demanded that the convention accept Zapata's Plan of Ayala, which, among other reforms, called for immediate land redistribution. Also, the Zapatistas made it clear that they were but an advanced party of a larger delegation. The Villistas supported the Zapatistas to a man.[20]

Carranza's position was awkward. If he attended the convention, he would be acknowledging its legitimacy. However, the convention seemed to be marching inevitably toward his removal as First Chief. Carranza sent a letter to the convention that was read to the delegates by Obregón on October 29. Carranza accused some of the delegates of being "reactionaries," claiming that he was too radical for them. Carranza wrote that he *would be disposed* to retire as first chief *if* Villa and Zapata retired. This circuitously worded letter threw the convention into chaos.[21]

Even though the Carrancistas still held the majority at the convention, on November 1, the body elected Gen. Eulalio Gutiérrez as interim president at the suggestion of Obregón. Gutiérrez was acceptable to all factions, in part because he was too weak to effectively deal with any one of them. Prior to the revolution, he had worked at menial jobs. He had fought for Madero and later against Huerta. Gutiérrez was justly known for his honesty. He was tasked to maintain order and hold national elections. Obregón headed a delegation sent to Mexico City to inform Carranza that his evasively worded resignation had been accepted.[22]

Carranza appreciated that Mexico City was far too vulnerable because of the nearness of his sworn enemies; Villa's army had moved into northern parts of the state of Aguascalientes, and the Zapatistas doggedly plagued areas just south of the capital. Carranza abandoned Mexico City on November 1, slowly retreating by rail toward Veracruz, which was still in the hands of the American invaders.

Carranza had to have been concerned over the loyalty of Obregón. Obregón's actions in Chihuahua City and at the Aguascalientes Convention could easily have been interpreted as hostile toward Carranza. In fact, generals Alvaro Obregón, Lucio Blanco, Pablo González, Antonio Villarreal, and Eduardo Hay, after leaving Aguascalientes ostensibly to tell Carranza that his half-hearted resignation had been accepted, met in Silao (175 miles northwest of Mexico City) to decide their future actions. They were aware that Villa's army was moving south toward Mexico City. Obregón revealed their decision; it was not so much for Carranza as it was against Villa. The generals insisted that Villa retire, and should he not, they would fight him. The generals stated that Villa needed to be sent outside the country—perhaps in a diplomatic position. When this was done, they would obtain Carranza's retirement and his departure from Mexico. But the convention could not restrain Villa. Thus on November 19, Obregón declared war on Pancho Villa and then followed Carranza toward Veracruz, which the Americans had evacuated on November 23.[23]

On December 1, Villa halted his army at Tacuba, five miles north of Mexico City, to be sure not to enter the city without first discussing the occupation with Zapata. The Zapatistas quietly filtered into Mexico City in small numbers and proved to be anything but the barbaric hoards that the city dwellers had feared. When their meager supplies ran out, they politely begged from the populace. The one exception was horses. These they "liberated" at every opportunity, frequently leaving owners marooned with their now horseless carriages.[24]

Zapata, an extremely cautious man for good reason, agreed to meet with Villa at Xochimilco, twelve miles south of Mexico City, the vicinity of which was under his control. With typical boldness, Villa rode to the meeting place escorted by only a few *Dorados*. He and Zapata met on December 4, 1914. There these two powerful, yet politically ignorant, *caudillos* cursed Carranza—a subject they could readily agree upon—and told each other war stories.

Next, Villa and Zapata disposed of some practical business. Each had under his protection a few old enemies of the other. In this environment of survival of the fittest, lesser *caudillos* sought new patrons when their old liege had been eliminated by a more powerful *caudillo*. A few enemies of Zapata had found haven in Villa's domain, and vice-versa. Zapata requested the surrender of Guillermo García Aragón, and Villa consented. Villa asked for three Orozquistas, including Benjamín Argumedo. Following the defeat of Huerta, some Orozquistas who had been fighting for him had aligned themselves with Zapata. Zapata refused to give Villa these men, stating that he had given his word to them, but in their place he offered others.[25]

Next, they dealt with the strategy to defeat Carranza, an undertaking neither perceived to be too arduous. After all, Carranza was a mere politician, most of Obregón's subordinate *caudillos* had deserted him, and González had retreated to the mountains of Huasteca. Villa and Zapata decided to split their forces. Zapata would drive through Puebla and ultimately to Veracruz. Villa would eliminate opposition in the north and approach Veracruz via Apizaco. Zapata complained of a lack of weapons, particularly artillery, and munitions. Villa promised to supply both.[26]

In the lateness of the day, they felt forced to say something about their political goals, although they would have been much happier continuing to regale each other with stories of their campaigns. Villa said, "I understand very well, that we ignorant men fight the wars and the cabinets have to put them to use. . . ." Later he said, "When I can really see where my country is going, I will be the first to retire, so that you can see we're honorable men, that we've worked like real men of the people, that we're men of principle."[27] In other words, Villa and Zapata declared no governing political goals to their action but rather, they would know the proper outcome when it occurred. This was hardly a position that would attract new followers or international recognition.

On December 6, fifty thousand revolutionaries, mostly Villistas and Zapatistas, paraded through Mexico City. The next day Villa and Zapata met again, this time in Mexico City at the National Palace. Eulalio Gutiérrez was also present, since the Aguascalientes Convention had made him the interim president. Zapata left Mexico City on the 9, taking with him reinforcements and artillery provided by Villa. The two would never again meet.[28]

In spite of Villa's agreement with Zapata, Angeles counseled Villa to immediately attack Carranza in Veracruz before Obregón could organize an army. Angeles argued that holding Veracruz gave Carranza access to considerable revenues and that Zapata was incapable of taking the port. Instead, Villa chose to consolidate his hold over the north, arguing that Veracruz was within Zapata's domain, but should he fail to capture the port, Villa would show Zapata how to do it. Villa decided to send General Angeles to attack General Antonio Villareal at Monterrey and generals Tomás Urbina and Manuel Chao to attack General González at Tampico; Villa would attack generals Manuel Diéguez and Francisco Murguía at Guadalajara.[29]

Obregón also appreciated the importance of Veracruz and anticipated not only being attacked but also being defeated. He personally scouted an escape route to Salina Cruz on the Pacific Coast across the Isthmus of Tehuantepec.[30]

Left in Mexico City without the counsel of some of his ablest advisers, Villa chose this time to even some old scores. The most blatant violation of authority were the murders of David Berlanga and Paulino Martínez, members of the Aguascaliente Convention, by Villa's personal assassin, Rodolfo Fierro. Berlanga had frequently criticized Villa, calling him a bandit and worse. Apparently, Martínez' chief offense was writing an article criticizing Franciso Madero, whom Villa idolized. In addition, some two hundred Mexicans were gunned down in the city, many at the direction of either Villa or one of his henchmen.[31]

Zapata's campaign against Carranza opened with blazing success. The Zapatistas took Puebla within weeks. But here Villa's and Zapata's strategy began to unravel. Zapata's peasant farmers had reached "the end of the earth." To go farther would carry them too far away from the small plots of land they believed their battlefield victories had secured for them. Now, they only wanted to return home and defend their land—southern Mexico—against invasion. Within a matter of weeks, Villa had lost his once-promising ally and had to face Carranza alone.[32]

But all was not lost. Villa and Zapata controlled central Mexico from the border with the United States beyond Mexico City into the deep south. Villa also had access to American munitions through Ciudad Juárez. And in addition, Villa commanded some sixty thousand troops, admittedly, many of them scattered throughout the vast territory he controlled. Carranza held Veracruz, Tampico, the northeast frontier with the United States, and some of the west coast. At Veracruz, he collected five million dollars a month from import and export tariffs. Also, controlling Veracruz permitted Carranza to import American arms by sea more easily than Villa could haul them overland by rail. Moreover, controlling Tampico gave him access to oil revenues, which, because of World War I, were rapidly increasing.[33]

During this time, Villa carefully played "the American card." The most serious problem was fighting at the border town of Naco, Sonora. Here the Villista Maytorena and the Carrancistas Calles and Hill were warring for control of the northwest. Hill and Calles had dug in with their backs to the border, and the two sides began exchanging fire in mid-October. Artillery shells and small arms fire fell into the United States, causing deaths, casualties, and property damage in Naco, Arizona. In fact, this was an extension of the same rivalry that had caused Obregón to go to Chihuahua back in September 1914 and negotiate with Villa.

Villa was determined to resolve this matter by force and decided to send eight thousand troops led by General Juan Cabral, now a Villista. From an American perspective, this would only increase the threat to American lives and property. Therefore the U.S. secretary of state requested that Villa meet with General Hugh Scott, chief of staff of the U.S. Army, who had commanded the Southern Department for five years and developed a personal friendship with Villa.[34]

On January 9, 1915, Villa and Scott met in the center of the International Bridge that spanned the Rio Grande between El Paso, Texas, and Ciudad Juárez, Chihuahua, and agreed to continue the meeting in Ciudad Juárez the next day. After two hours of discussions, Villa, wanting to appease the Americans, finally agreed to Scott's proposal that the area around Naco, Mexico, be neutralized. The Carrancistas would evacuate the town; the Villistas would withdraw westward; and Naco would be closed to military traffic.[35]

Throughout this period, Villa agreed to most requests from the American consul, George Carothers. Villa hoped that through courteous treatment of American representatives, diplomatic recognition of his government would follow; at this time, President Woodrow Wilson still thought more highly of Villa than Carranza.[36]

In Veracruz, Carranza, the consummate politician, adopted many of Zapata's agrarian reforms in order to win new followers, even though they contradicted previous statements he had made. On January 6, 1915, he reinstated the *ejidos*. This nullified the land concessions to the large landholders made during the Porfirio Díaz dictatorship. A month earlier, Carranza decreed support for the fledgling labor movement, thus winning additional supporters.[37]

While Carranza was attending to political matters, Alvaro Obregón was organizing his army. Villa had withdrawn his army north of Mexico City and Zapata had left only a weak garrison in Puebla, some 125 miles from Veracruz. This gave Obregón significant freedom to build his army and advance on Puebla virtually undetected. His twelve thousand troops reached the outskirts of the city on January 4. After twenty-four hours of hard fighting, the poorly supplied Zapatistas withdrew from Puebla.[38]

On January 11th Carranza telegraphed Obregón suggesting that he immediately attack Mexico City. However, this was a larger risk than Obregón wanted to take. Numerous factions remained in the city, and should they unite, it was not clear that Obregón would be victorious. Instead, Obregón conspired to separate Gutiérrez, who was still the Aguascalientes Convention's interim president, from Villa and Zapata. Obregón sent the confidential telegrams exchanged between him and Gutiérrez to Carranza, and unfortunately for Gutiérrez, much of their contents was released to the press.

While Villa was in the north negotiating with General Scott, he received confirmation of Gutiérrez's intrigues with Obregón through General Felipe Angeles. On January 5 Angeles had defeated the Carrancistas led by Antonio Villarreal at Ramos Arizpe (1,050 miles northwest of Mexico City). Villarreal's flight was so precipitous that he abandoned many confidential papers.

Villa traveled south from the border to Monterrey where he met with Angeles who displayed the evidence of Gutíerrez's communications with Carranza. Villa was furious and, on January 15, telegrammed General José Robles, an officer in the Division of the North who was in the capital, to execute the interim president. Instead of following Villa's orders, Robles told Gutiérrez, who fled the capital for San Luis Potosí, taking with him thirteen million pesos from the treasury to finance future military operations. Constantly harassed as he retreated northward, Gutiérrez's followers deserted him. He did not renounce the interim presidency until June 2, 1915.[39]

With Gutiérrez' departure from the capital, the Villistas and Zapatistas called a conference, deposed Gutiérrez, and named Roque González Garza as provisional president. Mexico thus had three interim presidents—Carranza, self-proclaimed on August 20, 1914, after the signing of the Teoloyucán Convention; Eulalio Gutiérrez, chosen by the Aguascalientes Convention on November 6, 1914; and González Garza, elected by the Mexico City Convention on January 15, 1915, under orders from Villa.

Now Villa decided to abandon Mexico City, which was still occupied by the Zapatistas, to its fate. The campaign in the north was not going well. As initially planned, Villa's subordinates were to win the northeast and he was to win the west. In fact, Villa was diverted from the western campaign to deal with U.S. protests over the fighting along the border and the defection of Gutiérrez. So Villa gave the command of the western campaign to generals Rodolfo Fierro and Calixto Contreras. Both men were brave fighters but neither was a strategist nor even a good tactician.[40]

On January 17 and 18, the Carrancista generals Diéguez and Murguía, attacking without artillery, surprised Fierro and Contreras and drove them out of Guadalajara, Mexico's second largest city, and back to Irapuato. As a result, Villa stripped Mexico City of his remaining five thousand troops and moved northwest by train. González Garza warned him that the capital would be lost. Villa responded, "It is important to win battles in war and then let the battles provide the prestige and deliver the cities."[41]

Villa joined with Fierro and Contreras and, with the eleven-thousand-man Villista army, entered Guadalajara without a fight. On February 18 Villa defeated eleven thousand Carrancistas near Sayula in a day-long battle. But once again Villa was pulled away to deal with the Carrancistas who were threatening Angeles at Monterrey. Before departing, Villa stopped Fierro from shooting all the prisoners, pointing out that the men were needed to repair the rail lines.[42]

With both Gutiérrez and Villa abandoning the capital, Carranza had ordered Obregón to immediately reoccupy Mexico City. The Zapatistas chose not to fight and left the capital. Further, those members of the Aquascalientes Convention who had moved to the capital chose to flee southward. On January 28 Obregón's Constitutional Army of Operations marched into Mexico City.[43]

Mexico City now became a city under siege: the Zapatistas agitated from the outside while the Carrancistas stripped it of its wealth from within. Carranza had no intention of holding the capital. He wanted to force the diplomatic corps to move to Veracruz to remove all that might be of value in his fight with Villa and to punish the city dwellers for supporting the numerous other factions. Whatever machinery could be taken was shipped to Veracruz. Obregón confiscated every private automobile and horse he could get his hands on.[44]

While this was going on inside Mexico City, the Zapatistas remained in the southern barrios. Although they would not engage in open battles—in large measure because of a shortage of munitions—they regularly harassed the Carrancistas. In addition, the Zapatistas cut off the city's food supply from the south and west and shut down its primary source of water.[45]

The dire straits of the poor in Mexico City made recruiting for Obregón's army easier. He was able to raise some nine thousand men—six battalions known as the "Red Battalions" because they were sponsored by the labor movement's "House of World Workers" (*Casa del Obrero Mundial*).[46]

Obregón, an agnostic, also took this opportunity to punish the Roman Catholic Church for its support of the conservative Victoriano Huerta regime. His soldiers sacked the city's wealthiest churches. As General Salvador Alvardo explained, "It was for the deliberate purpose of showing the Indians that lightning would not strike that generals rode their horses into the church and publicly smashed the statues of venerated saints."[47]

On February 12 Obregón demanded 500,000 pesos from the Church within five days; when this was not paid, he jailed 168 priests. The money was never paid. Eventually, many of the priests bought their freedom; an embarrassed Carranza freed the others. Obregón also taxed the wealthy, and if they did not pay, they, too, were jailed. Foreign governments protested to Carranza, but to no avail.[48]

Meanwhile in the north, Angeles, who had occupied Monterrey following his victory at Ramos Arizpe on January 5, was soon under threat from three directions. Gen. Eugenio Aguirre Benavides, who commanded in San Luis Potosí to the south of Monterrey, declared alliance to Convention-president Gutiérrez and thus came out against Villa. The Carrancista General González was to the east with a large army and General Herrera, whom Angeles had driven out of Monterrey, was to his north with the remnants of his army. Although Angeles's army now numbered about fifteen thousand men, the combined armies of his enemy were more numerous.[49]

Villa, bringing reinforcements, arrived in Monterrey on March 13th and ordered Angeles to go on the offensive. The Villistas defeated the Carrancistas the next day at Villareal. While at Monterrey, Villa extracted one million pesos from the city leaders, causing much ill will.[50]

Generals Urbina and Chao, whom Villa had tasked with taking Tampico, were faced with an unexpected problem. Aguirre Benavides's defection to Convention-president Gutiérrez meant that first they had to capture San Luis Potosí. They accomplished this and then moved eastward toward Tampico. On March 5 they arrived at the El Ebano fortification some forty miles west of the port. The Carrancistas were well supplied; the British oil company, El Aguila, had carried munitions from Galveston and New Orleans to Tampico for the Carrancistas. Also, the Carrancistas were well entrenched with heavy machine guns protected by barbed wire. The ten thousand Villistas attacked but could make no progress against the defenses. After sustaining heavy casualties, Villa ordered the withdrawal of all but a screening force because he needed the troops elsewhere.[51]

With Villa's absence from the west, once again the fighting did not go well. Following Diéguez' defeat by Villa near Sayula on February 18, Diéguez had fallen back on the port of Manzanillo and was resupplied from the sea. His six-thousand-man army then moved to Tuxpan. On March 22 Fierro attacked the well-dug-in Carrancistas at Tuxpan and was defeated, losing two thousand men and eight hundred horses. In addition, he had to abandon Guadalajara.[52]

Villa soon learned of Obregón's advance north by train out of Mexico City on March 11. Obregón used the eastern rail route and established a base at Tula (250 miles north of Mexico City) in an attempt to protect his avenues of retreat to Veracruz and Tampico. With Obregón's departure from Mexico City, the Zapatistas, accompanied by the Aguascalientes Convention now chaired by the Villista González Garza, immediately reoccupied the city.[53]

Angeles advised Villa only to harass the forces under Obregón while defeating those under González, which were protecting the Tampico oil fields. Angeles reminded Villa that Obregón was a cautious man and would not attack unless he possessed superior numbers. But Villa chose to attack Obregón. He reasoned that if Obregón moved too far north without being challenged, he would cut off the Villistas fighting in the west, particularly those in Jalisco.

Pancho Villa dressed in a general's uniform. He is wearing the Medalla de Valor given to him by the officers of the Division of the North on February 14, 1914, in Chihuahua City. Although Villa did not enjoy formal ceremonies, he did know how to dress for the occasion as evidenced by numerous photographs. When fighting with his men, he typically wore a collarless shirt, work pants, and boots.
Southwest Collection, El Paso Public Library

Porfirio Díaz became president of Mexico on November 28, 1876, and governed directly, or indirectly through puppets, until May 25, 1911. During his rule, Díaz evolved into the idol of the rich and the exploiter of the poor. Ironically, he had gained prominence as a Liberal while fighting for Benito Juárez during the 1860s.
Library of Congress

An undated photograph of Pascual Orozco (center, wearing light shirt and suspenders) and his men, probably taken early in the revolution. Orozco was the key architect of the victory at Ciudad Juárez that propelled Francisco Madero into the presidency. Beyond that success, Orozco had trouble choosing the winning side. In March 1912, he rebelled against Madero and was driven from Mexico by General Victoriano Huerta. In February 1913, he chose to support Huerta and was again driven from Mexico, this time by Pancho Villa.
Library of Congress

Mexican federal troops on the march in northern Mexico circa 1910. These men were well outfitted (they wear shoes rather than sandals) and appear to be carrying standard rifles.

U.S. National Archives

General Hugh Scott and Pancho Villa meet in 1913. The two men developed a close enough relationship that the U.S. Government frequently asked Scott to negotiate with Villa even after Scott was no longer assigned to the border region.
Southwest Collection, El Paso Public Library

Left to right: Villa's assassin Rodolfo Fierro, Pancho Villa, and fellow revolutionaries José Rodríguez and Juan García pose together at Ciudad Juárez in 1913.
Southwest Collection, El Paso Public Library

While Villista troop trains looked chaotic, they made use of every bit of available space. Typically, the men rode on top of the boxcars while their horses rode inside. Frequently, hammocks were hung under the cars between the wheels.
National Archives

Felipe Angeles was the man most responsible for creating a modern army out of Pancho Villa's large but irregular cavalry known as the Division of the North. A graduate of Mexico's Colegio Militar, Angeles was a recognized artillery expert who, between campaigns for Villa, was employed by the Allies as an ordnance inspector in World War I. Angeles was captured by the Carrancistas and shot on November 26, 1919.
Southwest Collection, El Paso Public Library

This frequently published photograph of Pancho Villa has been cited as being taken in March 1914 as he moved southward out of Chihuahua City to attack Torreón. It is more likely that the Mutual Film Corporation took it under an agreement with Villa's officers whereby they gave the company exclusive access to the battlefield in exchange for money to help outfit their men. If this is correct, the picture would have been taken in January 1914 during the Ojinaga Campaign.
National Archives

Francisco Madero and Abraham González—two of Pancho Villa's heroes, both of whom were assassinated by Victoriano Huerta— adorn this five-peso note issued by Villa. Villa's practice of issuing his own paper money particularly agitated Venustiano Carranza.
Author's collection

In addition to their more traditional role as camp followers, female combatants were quite common in the armies fighting in northern Mexico.

Southwest Collection, El Paso Public Library

Pancho Villa (center) and Alvaro Obregón (left), confer with General John Pershing (right), commanding general at Fort Bliss, on the International Bridge on August 27, 1914. In the second row from left to right are Lieutenant Colonel Francisco Serrano, Major Julio Madero (brother of the assassinated president), lawyer Luis Aguirre Benavides, and a U.S. first lieutenant who has been identified as both George Patton (future commander, U.S. Third Army in Europe during World War II) and James L. Collins (the future chief of staff of the U.S. Army and father of astronaut Michael Collins). It is probably Collins. *Southwest Collection, El Paso Public Library*

Venustiano Carranza rapidly evolved into Pancho Villa's archenemy. Carranza was aloof; Villa was gregarious. Carranza was an upper-class country squire; Villa was a lower-class bandit. Carranza was a politician and aristocrat; Villa perceived himself to be of the people. Carranza was educated; Villa was not. They were opposites in many regards, and they despised each other's attributes.
Library of Congress

In one of the most famous photographs of the Mexican Revolution, taken in December 1914, Pancho Villa sits in the presidential chair wearing a general's uniform and Emiliano Zapata sits to his immediate left. Seated to Villa's right is his loyal supporter, General Tomás Urbina. Seated to Zapata's left with the bandaged head is his supporter, General Otilio Montaño. The individual on the extreme left of Zapata wearing the hat and resting his hand on his belt buckle is Villa's assassin, Rodolfo Fierro. In 1915, Villa would have Fierro execute Urbina for making off with the war chest.
Casasola, Mexico City

Pancho Villa at the apex of his power in January 1915 in El Paso, Texas.
Southwest Collection, El Paso Public Library

A Carrancista battery prepares to fire on Villistas at the second battle of Agua Prieta in November 1915. Field artillery, the bane of Pancho Villa's military strategy, had undergone significant improvements during the latter part of the nineteenth century. Most important, the effects of recoil were reduced so that the guns could fire with greater accuracy.
National Archives

As in all revolutions, executions, like this one of Villista partisans by Carrancista forces in January 1916 at the Juárez railroad station, were common. Villa also routinely executed his enemies, including federal army officers, or those who were simply unfortunate enough to cross him on a "bad day."
Southwest Collection, El Paso Public Library

If such a thing as a winning *caudillo* existed in the Mexican Revolution, it would have to be Alvaro Obregón for, among the titans, he was the last man standing. Obregón possessed the skill of a mountain goat in his ability to walk the very narrow ledge between opposing camps and always know the correct moment to throw his support to one side or another. But unlike Villa, he was not the type of man who would be immortalized by the common folk in song. This is his wedding photograph taken in mid-1916. But like most of the strongmen of the Mexican Revolution, he, too, was assassinated. *Library of Congress*

The U.S. Punitive Expedition marches into Mexico. Perhaps the most important lesson of the expedition was how *not* to do things.
Southwest Collection, El Paso Public Library

In this photograph, Villa hardly looks like a bandit or a violent revolutionary. It is believed that it was taken after he had retired to his government-provided ranch in Sonora. *Southwest Collection, El Paso Public Library*

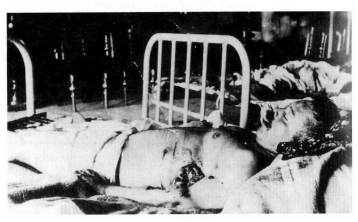

Villa lies dead on July 20, 1923. Grave robbers later dug up his body and stole his head. It has never been recovered. *Southwest Collection, El Paso Public Library*

Villa assembled his forces in Aguascalientes. He ordered Angeles to join him, but on April 2 while in Torreón, a horse fell on Angeles, severely injuring his foot. He could not walk or mount a horse, but he did manage to send an urgent telegram to González Garza in Mexico City urging him to have the Zapatistas attack Obregón's supply lines.[54]

Zapata agreed to attack the rail lines between Querétaro and Tula but was pessimistic about the outcome because of his shortage of munitions. Nevertheless, on April 3 González Garza telegraphed Villa at Aguascalientes that the Zapatistas had achieved a significant victory at Tula; unfortunately for Villa, this information was erroneous, although González Garza did not know that. Villa's 22,000-man army started south, and by April 4 he arrived at Irapuato. This placed Villa south of the railroad spurs that ran west and allowed him to protect the Villistas fighting in Jalisco. A day earlier Obregón's eleven-thousand-man army, traveling by rail toward the southwest, arrived at Celaya (130 miles northwest of Mexico City), thirty-five miles due east of Villa.[55]

Some twenty-five thousand inhabitants populated Celaya. It lay in a rich agricultural region known for its fruits. Drainage ditches crisscrossed Celaya's agricultural fields. This terrain was best suited for defensive warfare, and Obregón positioned his men in the irrigation ditches and protected them with rolls of barbed wire. The Carrancistas possessed a significant advantage in field pieces—thirty-five guns to the Villistas' twenty—and they had superior ammunition. The Villistas possessed only poor-quality shells manufactured in Chihuahua; the Carrancistas, for the most part, were using shells manufactured in Europe. This meant that the Villista guns would have to get close to the Carrancistas to have effect.[56]

Elements of Villa's army began arriving at Celaya on the 5th and spontaneously attacked as they encountered the Carrancistas. The only immediate option for attack was a cavalry charge since the infantry had not yet arrived and the artillery was still far away. Further dooming the early efforts of the Villistas was the fact that Villa himself, remained in Irapuato, where he was too far away to oversee the developing battle.[57]

Misjudging the concentration of Villa's forces, Obregón had dispatched his cavalry to the east, several days' ride from the battlefield. On April 6, Villa began a general assault. He defeated an element of Obregón's army at El Guaje, twelve miles from Celaya; only Obregón's arrival prevented a complete rout, which could have spread through the entire army.[58]

Villa rushed forward. At 5 p.m., Villa's rapidly advancing cavalry came upon Obregón's well-prepared defensive lines at Celaya. Without waiting for artillery and infantry, Villa's cavalry charged the fortified line throughout the remainder of the 6th and into the morning of the following day. Villistas led by Col. Pedro Bracamonte penetrated the center of Celaya where they climbed a church tower and rang the bell, prematurely declaring victory. But the Villistas ran out of ammunition and were soon driven from the town.[59]

Obregón sent the following telegraph to Carranza:

I am honored to inform you that the battle continues. The [enemy's] cavalries have been defeated. At this time, 11 p.m., we have suffered two thousand casualties. Enemy attacks are severe. You can rest assured that while I have a soldier and a bullet left, I well know how to do my duty and will consider it an honor if death should surprise me while fighting crime.[60]

Back in Veracruz, Carranza gathered up scattered units and rushed them to Obregón. On the 7 Villa attacked with his entire army without holding any forces in reserve. General Agustín Estrada led the cavalry attack on the right, but was foiled by flooded fields. Further, the infantry attack in the center was uncoordinated. After severe fighting, the Villistas were pushed back and their spirit waned.

At noon the Carrancista cavalry double-enveloped the Villistas. Villa's fatigued troops fought their way through the enemy's cavalry; however, their retreat soon became a rout. The Carrancistas lost 557 killed; 365 were wounded; the Villistas lost eighteen hundred killed, three thousand wounded, five hundred prisoners, and a large quantity of material. In particular, Villa's elite *Dorados* sustained very heavy casualties. The first Battle of Celaya was a Carrancista victory but it was not decisive.[61]

The Villistas fell back to Salamanca. Villa gathered up those reinforcements immediately available, bringing his army to twenty-five thousand men. He reorganized, but was too impatient to wait for Angeles and the additional artillery. Obregón dug in and received significant reinforcements, raising his army to fifteen thousand men. General Benjamín Hill commanded the seven thousand infantry; General Cesáreo Castro, the eight thousand cavalry; and German soldier of fortune Colonel Maximilian Kloss, the thirteen field pieces. In addition, Obregón possessed eighty-six machine guns.[62]

The Second Battle of Celaya began on April 13 at 5 p.m. in a heavy rainstorm. Villa opened the fighting with an artillery barrage—some thirty guns, mostly 75 and 80 mm; yet half of his artillery and Angeles' were still absent. Within an hour, Villa's cavalry was recklessly charging Obregón's well-entrenched infantry. Again and again over two days, Villa's cavalry charged unsuccessfully, seeking a breakthrough. On the fifteenth Villa sent a strong cavalry detachment around Obregón's left flank that attacked Celaya from the east. But the Carrancistas held fast. Then Obregón took the offensive and caught Villa by surprise. After a stubborn defense, the Villistas retreated. Once again the Carrancista cavalry double-enveloped the Villistas. This time Obregón possessed enough strength to crush the encircled, demoralized Villistas. The Carrancista victory was complete. Obregón lost 138 dead and 276 wounded. Villa lost 4,000 dead, 5,000 wounded, 6,000 prisoners, all of his artillery, and most of his supplies.[63]

Villa retreated north, tearing up railroad tracks behind him in order to delay Obregon's advance. Villa sought reinforcements and advantageous ground for a decisive battle. He recalled his troops fighting in Jalisco under generals Fierro and Contreras; he also ordered Chao to abandon the siege of El Ebano outside Tampico and join him at Aguascalientes. Angeles finally joined Villa from Torreón, bringing four thousand well-disciplined troops. Villa telegrammed his brother Hipólito in El Paso, Texas, to rush munitions to him, offering a bonus for the first shipment to reach him. Villa quickly rebuilt his army to thirty-five thousand men.

Obregón also prepared for the next encounter. Generals Francisco Murguía and Manuel Diéguez joined him from Jalisco, bringing with them eleven thousand Carrancistas. Obregón also received reinforcements from Carranza in Veracruz. Now Obregón commanded thirty thousand men who were well entrenched at Silao.

Once again, Angeles counseled Villa to abandon the offensive and fight defensively. He pointed out that Silao, like Celaya, was excellent ground to defend. It, too, was crisscrossed by irrigation ditches. He advised Villa not to attack but to draw Obregón farther from his base of support, Veracruz, and then cut him off from that support. But such a strategy was alien to Villa's nature. Villa told Angeles, "I am a man who came into the world to attack, and if I am defeated by attacking today, I will win by attacking tomorrow."[64]

The two sides began to clash daily on the plains of Bajío between the cities of León and Silao, which were about twenty miles apart. During forty days—April 27 through June 6—the fighting continued uninterrupted. On April 27, the Carrancista cavalry led by General Fortunato Maycotte advanced from Sauces toward León but were driven back by the Villistas. Two days later, Maycotte again tried to move forward but again was beaten back and retired to Silao. Next, Carrancista General Murguía attacked to the south and captured Santa Ana on May 3d. On May 6 and 7, Obregón advanced in the center and captured Trinidad, which he immediately fortified. Obregón's defensive line now ran southward from the hills around Otates, through Trinidad to Santa Ana in the south.[65]

Attempting to improve his reconnaissance, Villa acquired

three aircraft, but only one was serviceable and it crashed after a few days of service, killing the American pilot, Jack Mayes.[66]

On May 8 Carrancista General Diéguez went around the Villista north flank and on the twelfth captured Cerro de la Cruz (Hill of the Cross). Villa was furious. He unleashed cavalry charges against the position on the twelfth, thirteenth, and fourteenth, finally retaking the hill at a huge cost. The battle settled into an artillery duel, followed by infantry attacks into earthworks protected by barbed wire and machine guns.[67]

Now, typical of the recklessness that had won Villa victories at Ciudad Juárez on November 15, 1914, Tierra Blanca on November 24, 1914, and Paredón on May 17, 1915, he decided to risk everything on a single attack. During the evening of May 31, he led his entire eight-thousand-man cavalry through the hills in the north and attacked Silao from the east. Maycotte's cavalry fled back to Irapuato. Obregón's position was desperate. Murguía advised him to counterattack before his ammunition was exhausted, but Obregón insisted on a defensive strategy.[68]

On June 3, while observing the battlefield with his staff, a cannon shell almost tore off Obregón's right arm. Racked with pain, he put his revolver to his head. Some accounts say the gun misfired and others, that Obregón's aide had forgotten to load the revolver. At any rate, his staff restrained him and he was rushed to the first aid station at Trinidad where the arm was amputated.[69]

General Diéguez immediately assumed command and continued Obregón's defensive strategy throughout the day. On June 4 Generals Diéguez, Murguía, Hill, and Castro held a conference. Hill proposed that the hard-pressed Carrancistas retreat to Irapuato and reorganize. Diéguez agreed and Hill remained silent. Murguía argued that a retreat would be disastrous and they must attack. He said that he would attack León in the morning regardless of what the others did.[70]

On June 5 Murguía's cavalry attacked Villa's overstretched infantry in the center. Villa had withheld no reserves; his north wing had swung around behind the Carrancistas and could offer no support to the center. In the south, General Calixto Contreras's brigade had been supplied with faulty rifle ammunition; the brigade's rifles had little effect beyond fifty yards. This sealed Villa's defeat. By noon the Villista infantry broke and ran, abandoning their artillery and supplies. The Villista army disintegrated. By noon, Murguía had entered León.[71]

Villa decided to make a last stand at the city of Aguascalientes (364 miles northwest of Mexico City), eight miles north of León. Angeles argued against this. He advised Villa to retreat north into Chihuahua, tearing up the tracks behind him. Villa, once again, ignored Angeles's advice. There, on July 10, Villa lost 1,500 dead and wounded, 2,000 prisoners, 5,000 deserters, 8 trains, 33 locomotives, 4 million cartridges, 9 cannons, and 22 machine guns. The Division of the North ceased to exist. The Carrancistas lost only some 600 men.[72]

While the fight raged between Villa and Obregón to the north of Mexico City, living conditions in the capital continued to deteriorate. While the city remained under Zapatista control, they, for the most part, were powerless to alleviate the suffering of the people. These conditions fueled talk of intervention by the United States. To forestall such an event, Carranza finally decided to recapture the city. As Carrancista General Pablo González approached, the Zapatistas once again pulled out and González entered the capital on July 11, 1915. The long-dysfunctional Aguascaliente Convention dissolved. Once again, the Zapatistas cut off Mexico City's water supply.[73]

In the north, Villa still held hopes of recreating the Division of the North. To buy time he ordered a strong cavalry detachment commanded by Rodolfo Fierro and Canuto Reyes to circle behind Obregón and cut his communications with Veracruz. The Villistas surprised the Carrancistas at León, and they tore up the railroad. The Villistas then rode south, paralleling the tracks through Celaya, Querétaro, and San Juan del Río. In each town, the Carrancista garrisons retreated rather than fight. On July 17 the Villistas fought a sharp engagement with Carrancistas, commanded by Agustín Millán, at Tula. Millán withdrew to Pachuca, but there he was attacked by Zapatistas so he continued to retreat to Zempoala. This lay dangerously close to the key railway junction at Ometusco. As a consequence, General Pablo González abandoned Mexico City and moved north to protect this strategic town. For the last time, the Zapatistas reoccupied the capital. Eventually, the Villista raiding party, which briefly entered Mexico City, successfully worked its way north, having provided only a momentary scare.[74]

The Carrancistas would not be diverted from their pursuit of Villa. They captured San Luis Potosí on July 18, Querétaro on the twenty-eighth, Saltillo on September 4, and Torreón on the twenty-eighth. Torreón, which had cost so many Villistas their lives and was an important source of money, fell without a shot being fired.[75]

By now even the United States fully appreciated that Villa's star was setting, and it recognized the Carranza government on October 19, 1915. This recognition placed an embargo on arms to all revolutionary factions other than the Carranza government. In practical terms, this doomed any possible resurgence by Villa. He was enraged and sarcastically declared, "There is much I have to thank Mr. Wilson for, because he relieves me from the obligation of giving guarantees to foreigners and especially to those who had at one time been free citizens and are today vassals of an evangelical professor of philosophy. . . . I take no responsibility for future events."[76]

Villa's defeats at the hands of Obregón and Murguía may be attributed to many factors. Foremost were Villa's impulsive, wild cavalry charges at Celaya and his reckless gamble at León. These tactics had won the day against the reluctant armies of Porfirio Díaz and Victoriano Huerta but were the wrong tactics against the better-led Carrancista army. Second, Zapata may have been a kindred spirit to Villa but he was an impotent ally. Zapata was more the spiritual symbol of the *peons* in southern Mexico and less their *máximo caudillo*. He could not orchestrate control over his followers, in part because of his lack of arms and munitions. Third, Villa was fighting on too many fronts. He had forces tied down in the west from Jalisco to Baja California; in the north from Coahuila to Tamaulipas; and in the center from San Luis Potosí to Tampico. Villa's impulsiveness forced him to commit his army piecemeal against a numerically inferior, but well-commanded army.[77]

Chapter 5

Fighting "The Gringo" and "The New Establishment," 1916–20

V ILLA RETREATED NORTH, trying to salvage something from the crushing defeats; unfortunately, matters just got worse. To raise desperately need money, he levied new taxes and confiscated property. Despite these actions, the Villista currency plummeted from fifty cents on the U.S. dollar to five cents on the dollar.[1]

What is important to remember is that what "made" a *máximo caudillo* was his ability to reward his followers, and Villa was rapidly losing that ability. Valued old lieutenants deserted him. Tomás Urbina made off with the army's substantial war chest. This could not be tolerated—Villa, Fierro, and a few *Dorados* tracked him down at his ranch. Villa turned Urbina over to Fierro, "the butcher," with the instructions, "Dispose of him as you wish."[2] An even more crucial loss occurred on September 11, 1915, when Felipe Angles deserted Villa and rode off to self-imposed exile in the United States.[3]

Nevertheless, Villa would not quit, and he mounted another campaign. He dragged two batteries of artillery and thirty machine guns across the Sierra Madre Occidental Mountains and attacked *Carrancista* General Plutarco Elías Calles at the border town of Agua Prieta from November 1 through the 3. The Carrancistas, now recognized by the United States as the legitimate government of Mexico, rushed reinforcements by rail through U.S. territory. Obregón dispatched three infantry brigades by train from Piedras Negras across parts of Texas and New Mexico to Agua Prieta.

On November 1, Villa opened the battle by bombarding Agua Prieta from the east and west in order to prevent stray rounds from falling into the United States. Once again his cavalry charged and broke against barbed wire and artillery emplacements. Villa waited until dark and charged again. But searchlights illuminated the Villistas; they were powered by electricity supplied from the U.S. side of the border. These actions by the United States—the transportation of the Carrancistas and the supplying of electricity—enraged Villa.[4]

Villa's three thousand battered survivors marched west to Naco, another border town. There, the manager of the American copper company at Cananea sent two American medical doctors to treat the wounded. Villa accused the doctors of being spies, jailed them, and threatened daily to shoot them. Finally, the company paid Villa $25,000 in "taxes," and the doctors were released. One subsequently died from exposure.[5]

Villa then decided to march south and occupy Hermosillo, the state capital of Sonora. He hoped that the remoteness of this location would allow him time to rebuild his army. He sent funds to the *Villista* state governor, José Maytorena, to buy arms and supplies. Instead Maytorena fled to the United States, taking Villa's money with him.[6]

By the time Villa arrived at Hermosillo, the Carrancistas, led by General Diéguez, had already occupied the city. Villa attacked. On November 22, the outnumbered defenders were shuttled by cars from one side of town to the other for thirty hours and repulsed the uncoordinated and dispirited Villistas. As Villa retreated north, his army melted down to a few hundred men. Meanwhile Obregón had marched north and captured Chi-

huahua and Ciudad Juárez. General Villa, with no territory under his control, once again became Pancho Villa, the guerrilla.[7]

Also at this time, Villa lost his confidant and enforcer,
Rodolfo Fierro. Fierro was leading some Villistas from Ciudad
Juárez into Sonora. He insisted that his men ford Lake Guzmán
in order to save time. When they hesitated, Fierro rode forward
and his horse threw him. Weighed down by a money belt filled
with gold, he drowned in quicksand.[8]

Acts of violence by the Villistas against Americans increased.
A few Villistas crossed into the United States and threatened
American citizens. Before abandoning Ciudad Juárez on December 21 to the Carrancistas, the Villistas fired into El Paso,
Texas, killing a railway inspector. In spite of these incidents,
many Americans began to return to their commercial activities
in the northern Mexican states as the Carrancista government
seemed to be increasingly in control and capable of guaranteeing
their safety.

On January 19, 1916, about seventy Villistas stopped a train
near Santa Isabel; the train was steaming south to Chihuahua
City from the American border. They executed seventeen American employees, including the general manager, of the Cusi Mining Company; one escaped. Villa immediately claimed that the
Villista in charge, Colonel Pablo López, had exceeded his authority. Carranza, who feared an American intervention, un-
characteristically expressed regret and promised that the killers
would be caught. American citizens in El Paso protested against
Villa, and martial law had to be declared when mobs moved toward the Mexican quarter of the town.[9]

The killings at Santa Isabel were followed by Villa's four-hun-
dred-man raid into the United States. Villa planned to cross the
border near Ojinaga to the east of El Paso, but some of his men
deserted and he feared they would reveal his plan. Instead, Villa
crossed the border to the west of El Paso near Columbus, New
Mexico. Columbus lies seventy-five miles west of El Paso, Texas,
and two miles north of the border with Mexico. Columbus was
a poor, remote, isolated town. It had no electricity or telephones

but more than its share of rattlesnakes. It was the headquarters of the U.S. 13th Cavalry regiment, which comprised some 550 officers and men.[10]

Villa rode out of San Geronimo, Chihuahua, on February 27. While riding north, the Villistas caught and hanged three Americans so they would not spread the alarm. However, a ranch hand of the Palomas Company, Juan Favela, did see Villa's movement, rode ahead, and reported it to Colonel Herbert Slocum, commander of the 13th Cavalry Regiment. However, this contradicted other intelligence Slocum had received that same day, which indicated Villa was riding south. Slocum chose to ignore Favela's information, and the garrison took no extra precautions that night.

Villa crossed the border two-and-a-half miles southwest of Columbus. At 1 a.m. on March 9, an American sentry challenged the Villistas as they entered Columbus from the west. They shot the sentry, mortally wounding him. The startled American soldiers frantically tried to arm themselves, but their weapons were locked up; the officers, who were not present, had the keys. Finally, the soldiers broke into the armory. Almost immediately, a melee ensued between the Villistas and the American soldiers and those American citizens who could find weapons.

The Villistas were particularly interested in the Mercantile Store and the Commercial Hotel, owned by Sam Ravel. It was rumored that Ravel had taken Villa's money but had not delivered the paid-for weapons and supplies. Fortunately for Ravel, he was away in El Paso. The Villistas ransacked the store and then marched on the hotel. There, stray bullets hit two drums of gasoline stored in the basement, which started a fire that soon spread to nearby buildings. The flames illuminated the Villistas, and they came under heavy weapons fire from the American troops who had finally gotten themselves organized. At dawn the Villistas retreated; Troop H, commanded by Major Frank Tompkins, was in hot pursuit.

Troop H overtook Villa's rearguard formation three hundred

yards south of the Mexican/American border. The Villistas abandoned their position and retreated for a mile before stopping. Tomkins received permission from Slocum to proceed deeper into Mexico. He again charged the Villistas, and they again withdrew. Soon Tompkins was fifteen miles into Mexico, and the main body of the *Villistas* turned and attacked his force. Heavily outnumbered, Tompkins withdrew. He had not lost a single man.[11]

For the United States, the Columbus raid resulted in the deaths of eight soldiers and ten civilians plus the wounding of six soldiers and two civilians. Villa lost somewhere between seventy-five and one hundred men. He did capture thirty mules, some horses (probably equal to the number lost in the fighting), three hundred Mauser rifles, and some military equipment. However, much of this was abandoned as he was chased south. Villa never explained his rationale for attacking Columbus. Undoubtedly, it was influenced by the United States politically abandoning him for Carranza.[12]

Pressured by American public opinion, President Woodrow Wilson had no choice but to act. He ordered a large military expedition to invade Mexico with the sole task of capturing Pancho Villa, while respecting Mexico's sovereignty—the two goals obviously in contradiction to one another. Attempting to claim the "high moral ground," Carranza wrote to Wilson expressing regret at Villa's actions. He also reminded Wilson of the inability of the United States to prevent the Indian raids from the United States into Mexico led by Gerónimo in 1880 and Victoria in 1884 and 1885. Carranza suggested that should Villa's raid be repeated, the Mexican government would agree to some kind of reciprocal arrangement whereby military forces from either side could cross the border. Wilson ignored this politically unacceptable proposal.[13]

The American Army was marginally prepared to undertake the Villa pursuit. Since the enacting of the Constitution in 1789, the U.S. Army had been a frontier garrison force. In times of war—1812, 1846–48, 1861–65, and 1898—the government mobilized citizens and created volunteer units which became the government's main fighting force. For the most part, the small regular army had preserved its identity apart from the wartime volunteers. The Mexican Revolution had caused two mobilizations of America's citizen army, one in 1911 and the other in 1913. These gathered together regular troops from frontier garrisons and called citizen soldiers to service. Much was learned from these previous mobilizations, and the experience permitted the Villa pursuit expedition to move out so quickly.[14]

John "Black Jack" Pershing was chosen to lead the expedition. As a young lieutenant, he had campaigned in northern Mexico chasing the Apache chief, Geronimo. He had fought in both Cuba and the Philippines. Pershing served in the 10th Cavalry Regiment, one of the units where enlisted men were blacks, hence the nickname "Black Jack." When selected to lead the Villa expedition, Pershing was the commandant of Fort Bliss on the outskirts of El Paso, Texas.

On March 15, only six days after Villa's raid, the Pershing Expedition began moving south in two columns. The strategy was to catch Villa between them. The four-thousand-man eastern column departed Columbus heading due south and crossed the border near Palomas, Mexico. The local Carrancista commander threatened to fight, but then chose not to. The two-thousand-man western column led by Pershing crossed the border fifty miles west of Columbus. The two columns were to converge at the Mormon settlement, Colonia Dublán, about 125 miles into Mexico.[15]

A major logistical problem arose when Carranza refused to permit the Americans the use of the Mexican railway system. Since the mules ate the entire contents of the wagons they were pulling within two hundred miles, the 125-mile journey left little space for fodder for the cavalry, munitions, and sustenance for the troops. In order to solve the supply problem, the army purchased two hundred trucks. Soon the wheel ruts, which marked the way from the border to Colonia Dublán, evolved into a crude dirt road.[16]

The conditions confronted by those in the expedition were miserable—an inhospitable terrain plus ninety-degree days and below–thirty-two degree nights. But, these were the same harsh conditions that had forged Pancho Villa. Many of the items supplied by the army proved to be ill suited to the campaign. Guns did not fit holsters and leather accoutrements for the animals were poorly designed.[17]

The western column reached Colonia Dublán first. There Pershing learned that Villa had retreated southeast to the town of San Miguel. Pershing immediately dispatched three lightly equipped, fast-moving columns. But Villa had not lingered at San Miguel and had moved farther south. On March 28, three hundred Villistas attacked and defeated the Carrancista garrison at Guerrero. Unfortunately, during the fight a bullet hit Villa's right leg, shattering his shinbone. The wound was very painful and immobilized Villa.[18]

Luckily for Villa, he left Guerrero that night by carriage. The 676-man American cavalry column led by Colonel George Dodd had pressed on relentlessly, covering 225 inhospitable miles at an elevation of 7,000 feet in one week. The column fell on the Villistas at Guerrero during the morning of the twenty-ninth. The Villistas, having spent the night celebrating, were surprised and badly beaten. Thirty Villistas were killed and five Americans wounded. More important, Villa's force was scattered and remained so without Villa to reunite them. The exhausted condition of the American horses prevented Dodd from immediately pursuing the wounded revolutionary.[19]

The American columns continued to search for Villa, but he could not be found. Initially, Villa hid in a cave high in the Sierra de Santa Ana. He was carried by burro into the mountains and raised by ropes into the cave. The entrance was camouflaged, and there his leg was attended, poorly, while he hid for six weeks. In the meantime, the searching American columns began exchanging shots with the local Mexicans, who were becoming increasingly agitated by their presence.

On April 12, a serious incident took place at Hidalgo del

Parral. A U.S. cavalry column commanded by Major Tompkins entered the town over the objections of its mayor, and a crowd of citizens gathered. Two shots were fired, and two American soldiers fell dead. The crowd then rushed the Americans, who opened fire. More than fifty Mexicans were killed or wounded. As a consequence, Pershing decided to concentrate his force between Guerrero and Chihuahua City in an attempt to avoid additional confrontations with the Mexicans.[20]

As a result of the Hidalgo del Parral and other debacles, representatives of the two governments met at the end of April; each had its own agenda. The Mexicans wanted an immediate withdrawal of the American troops, and the United States wanted Villa. The talks took place in Ciudad Juárez and El Paso. Representing the Mexicans was Alvaro Obregón, now secretary of war; representing the United States were generals Hugh Scott and Frederick Funston. Eventually Obregón and Scott hammered out an agreement. The Americans would gradually withdraw, and the Mexicans would increase their efforts to capture Villa. Woodrow Wilson agreed, but Venustiano Carranza would not since the agreement did not set a date for the American withdrawal.[21]

Hoping to further reduce the possibly of clashes with the Mexicans, General Funston ordered Pershing to concentrate his forces at the small town of San Antonio, Chihuahua, three hundred miles south of Columbus, New Mexico. Here during the month of May, Pershing's men got lucky. On May 5, 330 men of the 11th Cavalry surprised Villistas at a ranch named Ojos Azules (blue eyes), killing forty-four and capturing others. On the fourteenth Lieutenant George Patton, while buying corn in a village, killed General Julio Cárdenas, chief of the *Dorados,* plus three others. And on the twenty-fifth, a band of Villistas attacked an American hunting party; during the fight, the Americans killed Colonel Candelario Cervantes.[22]

While May was lucky for Pershing, June was not. General Funston ordered Pershing to fall back to Colonia Dublán. Now Pershing's patrols were not only searching for Villa, but also keeping an eye on the Carrancistas. On June 16 Carrancista General Jacinto Treviño warned Pershing that the only direction in which Pershing's troops would be permitted to move was north. Pershing responded that he recognized no such restriction. On June 21, Captain Charles Boyd, commanding 48 men from the 10th Cavalry, approached Carrizal, sixty miles east of Pershing's camp, in a threatening manner after having been refused entry by the local Carrancista commander. The 120-man garrison opened fire; twelve Americans were killed and twenty-three taken prisoner. The Mexicans sustained thirty-three casualties.[23]

The fight at Carrizal drove the United States and Mexico to the brink of war. The United States seized the bridges across the Rio Grande, mobilized additional National Guardsmen, and demanded the release of the twenty-three captives. Carranza, appreciating the seriousness of the situation, ordered the Americans freed on June 28. Pershing's new orders made him a virtual captive of his circumstance. He was forbidden to go more than one hundred fifty miles into Mexico. Morale now became Pershing's primary challenge, and the Carrancistas replaced the Villistas as his primary threat.[24]

But Pancho Villa would not wither away, and refused to become a broken man hiding like a wounded animal. He came down from his cave, eluded his enemies in spite of the fact that his leg never healed properly, and demonstrated the reckless courage that had produced many victories and had earned him the right to be a *caudillo máximo*. On September 16, Villa, leading eight hundred men, surprised and captured Chihuahua City. After freeing comrades from the local prison and making off with sixteen wagons loaded with munitions, he once again disappeared into the desert. On November 23, Villa reappeared and, after three days of hard fighting, again recaptured Chihuahua City. On December 7, the Carrancistas chased him out.[25]

Next the rejuvenated Villa brazenly descended on Torreón, capturing it easily on December 22 from Carrancista General Severiano Talamantes. Talamantes chose to commit suicide rather than explain the defeat to Carranza. Villa extracted a "loan" from the wealthy of Torreón and vanished as rapidly as he had appeared.[26]

Finally, the American and Mexican governments agreed on a withdrawal plan, and Pershing began moving north on January 30, 1917; he recrossed the border on February 5. The expedition had cost $130 million. Its greatest "accomplishment" was demonstrating how poorly prepared the American army was, as would soon become evident in the war in Europe.[27]

Now the fighting in northern Mexico became a contest between "Pancho the Rope"—the Carrancista general Francisco Murguía, who liked to hang his prisoners—and "Pancho the Pistols"—Villa, who shot his. On May 30, 1917, Villa surprised the Carrancista garrison at Ojinaga and for the second time (the first being in January 1914) drove his enemy across the Rio Grande into Texas. After stripping the town, Villa rode back into the desert.[28]

Villa attacked Chihuahua City on September 16. Murguía, possessing a much larger force, was waiting for him. Two hundred and fifty-six Villistas advanced too far and were captured. They were hanged along Columbus Avenue, one of the city's main roads.[29]

On November 20, Villa led one thousand followers back to Ojinaga and again drove the garrison across the Rio Grande, meeting little resistance. Again, he appropriated all he could haul away.[30]

Villa spent the first part of 1918 raiding isolated villages. Increasingly, he turned to kidnapping to finance his operations. Favorite targets were the Mormon colonists who had chosen not to follow Pershing when he withdrew from Mexico. Those who did not pay Villa were shot. In October he kidnapped American Frank Knotts, the owner of the Erupción Mining Company and demanded a $20,000 ransom. When Knotts's brother tried to pay the ransom in one-dollar bills, Villa refused to accept, complaining that they had pictures of "Gringos" on them. He demanded gold. This was paid, and Knotts was freed on November 18.[31]

With the dawning of 1919, Villa's prospects were becoming more favorable. Some 1,200 fighters now followed him. On December 11, Felipe Angeles crossed back into Mexico; he rejoined Villa at Tosesihua in January 1919. The artillery expert, still a warrior, was increasingly becoming an evangelist for social reform and reconciliation. Villa listened to him patiently but warned, "All that is well, general, but don't gringo-ize my people."[32]

Angeles advised Villa to attack the garrisons in the towns; Villa preferred to continue raiding small villages. Initially Angeles's strategy prevailed. On April 19, 1919, the Villistas attacked Hidalgo del Parral. The garrison fled, but the local militia retreated to a hill outside the town. Angeles persuaded them to surrender, promising that no reprisals would be taken against them. Villa honored the agreement. Nevertheless, there were opportunities for revenge. Male relatives of Maclovio Herrera, who had deserted Villa for Carranza, that lived in the town were hanged. The town was stripped, and a large sum of money extracted from foreign residents.[33]

Now Villa hoped to retrace his 1914 path to success. He would attack and capture the strategic border town of Ciudad Juárez. In late April, fifteen-hundred well-armed Villistas feigned an attack on Chihuahua City. Then they rode rapidly north, delaying only long enough to tear up almost fifty miles of track that connected Chihuahua City to Ciudad Juárez. They attacked the border town during the night of June 14, from the east to avoid stray bullets falling into Texas. The garrison fled. However, Villa lost control of his men, and while they were looting, the garrison regrouped and drove the Villistas out of Ciudad Juárez. Villa then took personal command and led the second attack; bullets were flying across the border. One American soldier was killed, and other Americans wounded.

While the fighting raged between the Villistas and Carrancistas, the American artillery on the north side of the Rio Grande began shelling the Villistas. Elements of the 5th and 7th U.S. Cavalry Regiments charged across the river and were followed by the elements from the 24th Infantry. Outnumbered and out-gunned, Villa retreated. Angeles wrote a letter of protest to the local U.S. commander, who responded that he need not explain his actions to Angeles.[34]

Following the defeat at Ciudad Juárez at the hands of the Americans, Angeles broke with Villa for a second and final time. The restless Angeles then sought to serve other *caudillos*, but became disillusioned; he was captured by the Mexican government, tried by court martial, and shot on November 26, 1919. Many prominent individuals of the international community appealed for mercy on behalf of Angeles, but to no avail. Angeles seemed resigned to the fact that his execution was a necessary part of a healing process for Mexico.

Villa's following once again dwindled to a small guerrilla band. On March 4, 1920, he blew up a train in the state of Chihuahua, killing the guards. Villa personally shot the two conductors and ordered the passengers to be lined up. Then with tears in his eyes, Villa told those about to be shot, "Since the execution of my friend General Angeles I have been thirsting for vengeance. That's why I blew up the train. Well, I have avenged his murder. Now, in memory of him I spare your lives. You may go."[35]

Following his defeats at the hands of Obregón in mid 1915 and early 1916, Villa once again demonstrated that he remained the master of guerrilla warfare. His brief military resurgence may be attributed to his knowledge of the region and the corruption of the Carranza administration; because of this corruption, inept officers like General Talamantes were given important commands. But this time the peasants did not flock to Villa's banner. Unlike 1913, Villa was not able to parlay his battlefield successes into national political stature. There were many reasons. Some were tired of fighting, while others hoped that the reforms promised by the Carranza government would materialize. Villa had lost his appeal.

Chapter 6

Fighting Forced Retirement, 1920–23

Time had not stood still in Mexico City during the years of cat and mouse between Villa and the government's troops.

In September 1916 Carranza called a constitutional convention at Querétaro. Not surprisingly, only those who were unwaveringly loyal to Carranza were elected. Of the 221 convention members, only 45 were military men. Carranza gave them a rewritten version of the 1857 Constitution, expecting the convention to rubber-stamp it. Like those at the Aguascalientes Convention before them, the delegates proved to be of independent mind and produced a liberal constitution that included the redistribution of land, the confiscation of church property, the ordaining of secular education, the granting of labor rights, and the limitation of foreign ownership. The convention even openly criticized Carranza. Perhaps learning from his experience with the Aguascalientes Convention, Carranza accepted the document and was elected president on March 11, 1917; he then chose to essentially ignore many of the provisions of the Constitution of 1917.[1]

Carranza implemented few of the promised reforms. Land was not redistributed to any meaningful degree, troops were used to break striking unions, education was neglected, the foreign debt went unpaid, and corruption was rampant. Numerous cronies were rewarded with commissions in the army. On April 10, 1919, Emiliano Zapata was assassinated. There was a tremendous lack of morality in public affairs. Carranza, ineligible for reelection in 1920 under the new constitution, tried to retain power through a puppet, Ignacio Bonillas, but was unsuccessful.[2]

In April 1920 Alvaro Obregón led a rebellion against Carranza. The rebels proclaimed the Plan of Agua Prieta, stating that sovereignty rested with the people and that Carranza had violated that sovereignty. Pancho Villa saw this as an opportunity to return to the winning side. Villa contacted Adolfo de la Huerta, one of the formulators of the plan, in an attempt to join the movement. De la Huerta had been one of the men who in April 1913 had given Villa enough money to launch an eight-man invasion of Mexico from the United States. Now he advised Villa to come to Hermosillo with a fifty-man escort. Next, Villa contacted Plutarco Calles, offering to fight against Carranza. Calles advised Villa to stop attacking towns and await orders.[3]

Calles authorized General Ignacio Enríquez, the recently appointed governor of Chihuahua, to negotiate with Villa. The two met but could not come to terms. Villa became suspicious of Enríquez's intentions and secretly abandoned the meeting site. Within hours, Enríquez attacked the abandoned camp. In revenge, Villa attacked Parral del Hidalgo on June 2, killing many.[4]

While these events were taking place, opposition to Carranza became overwhelming. He tried to escape from Mexico with five million pesos, but was caught and murdered. Although Alvaro Obregón was the man of the hour, six months remained on the term of the assassinated Carranza. One of the bedrock provisions of the new Constitution of 1917 was no reelection. Therefore, if Obregón served the remaining six months of Carranza's term,

the legitimacy of his election to a six-year term could be challenged. Obregón needed to find an individual he could trust to
be interim president. He chose Adolfo de la Huerta, the governor of Obregón's home state of Sonora, who easily won the secret ballot cast by the senators and deputies of Congress.[5]

De la Huerta, a banker and would-be opera singer, immediately endeared himself to a Mexico sick of violence by offering
reconciliation and reintegration to the many individuals who
had backed losing factions over the preceding ten years. De la
Huerta announced that those living in exile could return without fear of reprisals. He freed generals Francisco Murguía and
Francisco Mariel; they had remained loyal to Carranza in his recent contest with Obregón. De la Huerta offered land in exchange for peace to the Zapatistas, and most accepted.[6]

In the meantime, on July 10, 1920, Elías Torres, a close friend
of Villa and de la Huerta, delivered, to the interim president,
conditions upon which Villa would lay down his arms. Many of
those advising de la Huerta opposed compromise with Villa. On
July 26, 1920, Villa captured the town of Sabinas in Coahuila
from a seventy-man garrison. Villa then tore up the railroad
tracks north and south of the town to prevent a surprise attack.
He telegraphed de la Huerta, suggesting that he be given a hacienda and a bodyguard in exchange for his retirement. Hearing
of Villa's offer, Obregón voiced his strong opposition, but de la
Huerta, demonstrating a streak of independence rare among
"caretaker" presidents, ignored Mexico's real strongman.[7]

De la Huerta sent General Eugenio Martínez to Sabinas to
negotiate with Villa. On July 28 Villa agreed to surrender under
the following terms: (1) Villa would lay down his arms and retire
to private life; (2) the government would purchase for Villa the
25,000-acre Hacienda de Canutillo; (3) the government would
pay for fifty *Dorados* to serve as Villa's bodyguards; (4) the government would pay the remaining 759 Villistas one year's wages
at their current rank and grant them land where they wanted
(those wishing to join the Mexican army were inducted immediately); and (5) Villa would not take up arms against the

"Supreme Government." When pressed for an explanation of his actions by journalists, Villa responded, "You can say that the war is over; that now honest men and bandits can walk together."[8]

Considering the ranks that Villa had bestowed upon his followers, they were well rewarded. He, of course, was a general of division. Under him were 1 general of brigade, 23 colonels, 25 lieutenant colonels, 33 majors, 52 first captains, 33 second captains, 34 lieutenants, 41 sublieutenants, 31 first sergeants, 32 second sergeants, 14 corporals, and 480 soldiers.[9]

The government's terms were both generous and insightful. The Hacienda de Canutillo, located in the state of Durango, bordered on Villa's traditional stronghold—Chihuahua—but was not in it. Also, the hacienda was far from state capitals as well as rail lines; Villa was thus isolated from his traditional political base and means of rapid movement should he feel the call to action in the future.[10]

Now, a kinder, gentler Pancho Villa emerged. Those human qualities, which had fleetingly exposed themselves during the years of violence, fully bloomed. Villa demonstrated that his past articulations about the importance of hard work and education were not merely hollow utterances. He had told correspondent John Reed in 1914, "Honest work is more important than fighting, and only honest work makes good citizens."[11]

Villa profitably raised wheat, corn, and potatoes. He improved the infrastructure on his hacienda. He constructed a road from the ranch to Parral, the nearest town. Villa was also fascinated by the latest inventions of the day; for example, he imported the latest farming machinery.

But Villa's greatest love was education. He built a school on the hacienda for the children of his employees and bodyguards. He ordered that the windows be set high so the children would not while away their time by daydreaming about the outdoors. He paid for the sons of some *Dorados* to be educated in American military academies, and he paid for eight sons of his employees to go to business school in El Paso, Texas.[12]

Villa was frequently visited by the curious. Typical of his nature, he had forgiven the *gringos* for their role in his fall from power, even though the average American citizen had not forgiven Villa for his atrocities against their kinsmen.

Still, Villa did not tolerate fools lightly, regardless of nationality. When a photographer asked Villa to perform some cowboy tricks, Villa lost his temper and told him to leave his property.[13]

Moreover, the "Don Quixote" in his soul was never extinguished. When asked if he would ever fight again, Villa responded, only if Mexico were invaded by the United States or if Adolfo de la Huerta needed him. It was well known that in addition to the fifty *Dorados*, Villa could call on his numerous farm workers. He boasted of being able to raise 1,800 men if needed. Proudly, he displayed two Thompson submachine guns, which he claimed were gifts from his old enemy Alvaro Obregón.[14]

Pancho Villa lived in his "gilded cage" for almost three years, during which a number of attempts were made to assassinate him. Early on the morning of July 20, 1923, one finally succeeded. Villa was returning from the christening of one of his former *Dorados'* children when eight gunmen ambushed his Dodge automobile in Parral. Struck by seven bullets, Pancho Villa, age 46 years, was murdered. Accompanying Villa were his secretary, Miguel Trillo, himself killed by nine bullets, and four bodyguards. Two of the four bodyguards died immediately and another a few days later in the local hospital. The only survivor lost an arm in the ambush.[15]

The organizer of the killing was Jesús Salas Barraza, although he apparently did not take part in the shooting. He was arrested while trying to escape to the United States and sentenced to twenty years in prison. After serving six months, Salas was freed and made a colonel in the Mexican army. He died in 1951.[16]

Although no one has ever proven the government's involvement in Pancho Villa's death, the fate of Villa's assassin speaks volumes.[17]

Chapter 7

Conclusion

W HAT WAS PANCHO VILLA'S LEGACY to the Mexican people? Villa was one of the "titans" of the Mexican Revolution. Each of these titans—Porfirio Díaz, Francisco Madero, Victoriano Huerta, Venustiano Carranza, Alvaro Obregón, Emiliano Zapata, and Pancho Villa—possessed strengths and weaknesses. But the Mexican Revolution was more than a clash of titans—above all, it was a social revolution equal in magnitude to the Bolshevik experience. For the first time ever, the common Mexican was enfranchised with social, economic, and political rights. And in some measure, Pancho Villa must share in the credit of having given these rights to the average Mexican.

What was Pancho Villa's contribution to the Mexican Revolution? The young Liberal, José Vasconcelos, who lived through the upheaval, believed that in 1913 Villa saved the revolution. He wrote, "The revolution, threatened in Coahuila, also in Sinaloa due to the ineptitude of its Chief [Carranza], triumphed militarily thanks to the activity of the Division [of the North] created by Francisco Villa."[1]

How vicious was Pancho Villa? He was very vicious, but those were vicious times. Almost every revolutionary titan was assassinated—Madero, Zapata, Carranza, Obregón, and Villa. Between 1910 and 1920, the Mexican population decreased by 824,000 people, primarily because of the ferocity of the fighting, and to a lesser degree by people fleeing to other countries. Most of the titans of the Mexican Revolution—Porfirio Díaz, Victoriano Huerta, Venustiano Carranza, Alvaro Obregón, Emiliano Zapata, and Pancho Villa—ordered summary executions. Villa's seemed more numerous, and perhaps they were. One distinction was that Villa seldom made an effort to disguise that it was he who gave the order; and, clearly, he possessed the "backbone" to shoot a victim himself. The only titan who forgave his enemies was Francisco Madero. This cost him his life and also earned for him a saintlike status in the eyes of Villa.[2]

Who was the winner of the Mexican Revolution? Neither of the initial antagonists, Porfirio Díaz or Francisco Madero, was around at the finish. The confrontation soon took on a life of its own and became a revolution—a struggle among classes. Personified by Victoriano Huerta, the old guard failed to contain the forces of revolution. Villa and Zapata also failed to hold on to the "brass ring" after they had seized it. The fledgling bourgeoisie and the peasants failed to seize their opportunity. The winners were the pragmatic, industrious, self-made men from the north like Alvaro Obregón.

How was it that Villa most frequently won on the battlefield? The answer is simple. His followers were more willing to die for their leader than those fighting on the other side. During the Battle of Torreón in April 1914, correspondent John Reed wrote, "His name was a legend already with the enemy—wherever Pancho Villa appeared in battle, they had begun to believe it lost. And the effect on his own troops was also most important, too."[3]

In a society where few fighters comprehended the concept of nationality, the greater willingness of Villa's men and women to make the supreme sacrifice for him personally was his advantage. In early-twentieth-century Mexico, the ability to inspire your followers to great sacrifices was what made you successful.

How good a strategist was Villa? Pancho Villa possessed a fundamental, but hardly profound, understanding of national strategy. During his 1915 struggle against Carranza, he understood the need to secure and expand his base of power in the north. But he did not comprehend the critical importance of Veracruz, the initial vulnerabilities of Carranza, and Zapata's military limitations. Except for his mastery of speed and surprise, Villa's operational strategy almost always was the massed frontal assault. In a military sense, Villa was born too early or too late. The march of technology continually swings the battlefield advantage from the offense to the defense and back again. Villa was the master of the impulsive cavalry charge at the moment when field artillery, the machine gun, and barbed wire gave the advantage to the defense. Alvaro Obregón, Villa's chief antagonist, used these weapons to destroy Villa's cavalry. However, these new weapons did not have as much of an impact on guerrilla warfare as they did on the major battlefields, and in guerrilla warfare, Villa remained supreme.

What was Villa's contribution to the legacy of the Mexican military? Villa and other military "amateurs" like him destroyed the professional army and discredited the elite Mexican officer class. Villa, Obregón, and Zapata consistently defeated the reputedly professional soldiers. As a consequence, today the Mexican military traces its heritage to the 1910 revolutionaries and not to the traditional officer class.

And what were Pancho Villa's attributes? Villa was a classic *caudillo*. He was the toughest of the tough and attracted and held his followers by providing for their needs. Being the second toughest got you killed. Villa's secretary, Ramón Puente, wrote that he never stopped "once his hand had touched the handle of his pistol. . . ."[4] Bill Greet, the El Paso county clerk, observed, "Villa always had every faculty developed to the keenest degree. He seldom smoked, he never drank. He was one of the best shots I have ever known—*a sure shot*. He'd fight at the drop of a hat. A man knew that if he shot [at Villa] and missed he could count his death number right there and then."[5] General Hugh Scott wrote, "Villa had become quite temperamental in the use of his gun, which he carried always, pulling and using it suddenly, not always with sufficient cause, and the question was sometimes asked if his mind was functioning normally."[6]

For a few short years in the north of Mexico, Pancho Villa was the law. Villa was the interpreter and dispenser of justice. His ability to differentiate among evils was demonstrated by his decisions toward captured opponents. Captured federal soldiers who had been forced into the army were frequently turned loose. Yet he considered that captured *Colorados* (the followers of Pasqual Orozco) were fighting voluntarily against him and shot them. Captured federal officers were also shot because they were educated men and should have known better. But when angry, he would shoot anyone.[7]

Also, within his world he was admired for his conquests of the ladies. He married frequently, destroyed the documentation, and then rode off to another liaison. John Reed asked Villa if the stories of his amorous conquests were true. He responded, "I never take the trouble to deny such stories. . . . But tell me; have you ever met a husband, father, or brother of any women that I have violated? Or even a witness?"[8]

Villa's foremost qualities were his concern for the well-being of his soldiers, his regard for children, and his love of education. General Hugh Scott wrote, "I was told by the banker who handled his money that Villa had no fortune put away; that whatever he got he spent right away for food, clothing, and ammunition for his men, whom he took care of to the best of his ability."[9] During his brief one-month rule as the self-appointed governor of Chihuahua in January 1913, he started schools and hired teachers. At the height of his power, he paid for the education of hundreds of children.[10]

Villa thirsted for knowledge. He memorized parts of the 1857

Constitution, the Liberal document that had been ignored throughout the Porfiriato. Villa remarked, "It would be bad for Mexico if an uneducated man were to be President."[11]

The good and the bad of Pancho Villa are exposed in the character of his two close friends, Rodolfo Fierro, "the Butcher" (*el carnicero*), and Felipe Angeles, "Pancho's Angel." I. Thord-Gray observed, "At Villa's side stood, as always, Rodolfo Fierro who grinned sneeringly at me when Villa spoke."[12] Reed wrote, "During two weeks that I was in Chihuahua, Fierro killed fifteen inoffensive citizens in cold blood. But there was always a curious relationship between him and Villa. He was Villa's best friend; and Villa loved him like a son and always pardoned him."[13]

And then there was Villa's other friend, Felipe Angeles. M. L. Burkhead, who owned a car agency in El Paso, Texas, and knew Villa well, recalled, "Angeles was highly educated, gentle, brilliant. . . . The contrast with Villa could not have been greater, but Angeles joined with Pancho, becoming known as 'Pancho's Angel.' Villa never ceased to grieve [when Angeles died]. . . ."[14] Carl Beers, the representative of W. G. Roe Company of El Paso, recalled a conversation between Miguel Ortiz, a former soldier, and Villa in 1921 at his ranch. "Ortiz talked with Villa of the Revolution and mentioned Felipe Angeles. . . . Mention of Angeles evoked an emotional outburst from Villa. Tearfully he praised Angeles as a man of highest character and qualities. . . ."[15]

Why was it that Villa, who had escaped many an assassin's bullet and another's poison, was so easily ambushed in 1923? Villa had suspected everyone; typically he had kept his sleeping place a secret. Rarely had he eaten with his officers; rather, he would roam among his troops eating from their camp pots. But Villa possessed the *caudillo's* Achilles-heel—aging. As he grew older that animal instinct, which made him so successful, dulled, and he rode into the assassin's trap. One would like to believe that a younger Villa would have immediately recognized the danger signs and made his enemies pay for their audacity.[16]

Why was Villa's death almost anticlimactic? This was because by the time he was assassinated, he was no longer a great personage, merely an aging, retired bandit who had become "respectable."

And how did his contemporaries perceive Pancho Villa? Friends idolized Villa, and foes feared him. But all described him as possessing a wildness that dominated his soul.

Mercenary I. Thord-Gray, reflecting back to late 1913, wrote, "Villa was without a doubt a bundle of energy and strength willing to take grave risks to gain his objective, and he did so fearlessly."[17]

John Reed wrote in 1914:

> He [Villa] is the most natural human being I ever saw, natural in the sense of being a wild animal. He says almost nothing and seems so quiet as to be almost diffident. . . . If he isn't smiling he's looking gentle. All except his eyes, which are never still and full of energy and brutality. They are as intelligent as hell and as merciless. The movements of his feet are awkward—he always rode a horse—but those of his hands and arms are extraordinarily simple, graceful and direct. They're like a wolf's. He's a terrible man.[18]

Leon Canova, a U.S. Special Agent, wrote in late 1914, "When he [Villa] spoke to me of a break with Carranza and the preparations he was making for war against him, his face was illuminated with joy."[19]

Hugh Scott, who had negotiated with Villa on numerous occasions, wrote, "He was as unmoral as a wolf; nevertheless he had some fine qualities if you could reach them. . . . He never violated his compacts with me. . . ."[20]

John Pershing, who met Villa in August 1914 and would later chase him, wrote, "He was taciturn and restless, his eyes were shifty, his attitude one of suspicion. . . ."[21]

José Vasconselos, Mexico's future secretary of education who had escaped Villa's wrath, wrote that he was "a wild animal who in place of claws had machine guns and cannon."[22]

In spite of all his weaknesses, Villa will long be remembered, for today his name is more famous, or infamous if you prefer, than those who defeated and killed him. General Hugh Scott probably best summarized Pancho Villa. "Villa was a great sinner but had been greatly sinned against. He had the germs of greatness in him and the capacity of higher things under happier circumstances."[23]

Endnotes

Chapter 1

1. Enrique Krauze, *Mexico Biography of Power* (New York: HarperCollins, 1997), 307; Ernest Gruening, *Mexico and Its Heritage* (New York: D. Appleton-Century, 1934), 104; Friedrich Katz, *The Life and Times of Pancho Villa* (Stanford: Stanford University Press, 1998), 11–14.

2. Ruben Osorio, *The Secret Family of Pancho Villa: An Oral History* (Alpine, Tex.: Sul Ross University, 2000), 2–10; Krauze, *Mexico*, 306; Martín Luis Guzmán, *Memoirs of Pancho Villa*, trans. Virginia H. Taylor (Austin: University of Texas Press, 1975), 3–4.

3. Ramón Puente, "Francisco Villa," in *Historia de la revolución mexicana*, 2 vols. (Mexico: various, 1936), 1: 239–40; Jesse Peterson and Thelma Cox Knoles, *Pancho Villa* (New York: Hastings House, 1977), x; Guzmán, *Memoirs*, 4.

4. Krauze, *Mexico*, 307, 332.

5. Guzmán, *Memoirs*, 21–22; Krauze, *Mexico*, 308.

6. Robert E. Quirk, *The Mexican Revolution, 1914–1915* (New York: W. W. Norton, 1960), 3; Alfonso Taracena, *La verdadera revolución mexicana*, 12 vols. (Mexico: Editorial Jus, S.A., 1960–63), 1: 105–106; Jesus Romero Flores, *La revolución mexicana* (Mexico: Talleres Gráficos de la Nación, 1960), 30–31; Katz, *Life and Times*, 52–54.

7. George W. Crishfield, *American Supremacy*, 2 vols. (New York: Brentano's, 1908), 1: 221. For similar accolades from a senior U.S. Army officer, see Hugh Lenox Scott, *Some Memories of a Soldier* (New York: Century, 1928), 495–96.

8. Campbell's travel guide to Mexico notes:

   The police are not hard to find in Mexico as in some other countries, and there are soldiers everywhere; not as a menace,

but as a protection. Time was when bandits had their scenes
laid in Mexico . . . but that is ancient history. . . . There has
never been but one "hold up" of a passenger train in Mexico,
and that by American border thugs. Train robbers are ordered
to be shot on the spot of the hold up, and orders are obeyed
in Mexico.

Reau Campbell, *Campbell's New Revised Complete Guide and
Descriptive Book of Mexico* (Chicago: Rogers & Smith, 1907), 51;
Kurt F. Reinhardt, "Positivism in Mexico," *The Americas* 2, no. 1
(July 1945): 93–98.

9. Luis Garfías M., *The Mexican Revolution* (Mexico City:
Panorama Editorial, S.A., 1987), 11. Michel C. Meyer and
William L. Sherman, *The Course of Mexican History* (New York:
Oxford University Press, 1979), 466, place the Mexican popula-
tion at 15,160,000 in 1910.

10. Thomas A. Janvier, "The Mexican Army." *Harper's New Monthly
Magazine* 79, no. 474 (November 1889): 813–27, 827.

11. Guillermo Mendoza V. and Luis Grafías M., "El Ejército mexicano de 1860 a 1913," in *El Ejército mexicana* (Mexico: Secretaria
de la Defensa Nacional, 1979), 326–29; Francisco Bulnes, *The
Whole Truth about Mexico* (New York: M. Bulnes Book Co.,
1916), 146–47.

12. Moisés González Navaro, "Social Aspects of the Mexican
Revolution," *Journal of World History* 7, no. 2 (1964): 383.

13. Guzmán, *Memoirs*, 22–26; Taracena, *La verdadera revolución*, 1:
111; Krauze, *Mexico*, 308–309.

14. Krauze, *Mexico*, 309.

15. Mendoza and Grafías, "El Ejército Mexicano de 1860 a 1913,"
326; *Anales gráficos de la historia militar de México, 1810–1991*
(Mexico: Editorial Gustavo Casasola, S.A., 1991), 174; Daniel
Gutierrez Santos, *Historia militar de Mexico, 1876–1914* (Mexico:
Ediciones Ateneo, S.A., 1955), 50–51.

16. Guillermo Costa Soto, *Historia militar de México* (Mexico:
Impreso en los Talleros Gráficos de la Nación, 1947), 93:
Mendoza and Grafías, "El Ejército Mexicano de 1860 a 1913,"
329–31; Garfías, *Mexican Revolution*, 28; Ronald Atkin,
Revolution! Mexico, 1910–20 (London: Macmillan, 1969), 53.

17. Guzmán, *Memoirs*, 27.

18. Katz, *Life and Times*, 99; Jésus Romero Flores, *Anales históricos de la revolución mexicana,* 4 vols. (Mexico: El Nacional, 1939), 1: 153; Garfías, *Mexican Revolution*, 32; Atkin, *Revolution!*, 51–62.

19. Guzmán, *Memoirs*, 28–29; Taracena, *La verdadera revolución*, 1: 112.

20. Carleton Beals, *Porfirio Díaz*, (Philadelphia: J. B. Lippincott, 1932), 426; Atkin, *Revolution!*, 53.

21. Atkin, *Revolution!*, 56.

22. Guzmán, *Memoirs*, 38–39.

23. Beals, *Porfirio Díaz*, 426–27.

24. Romero, *Anales históricos*, 1: 70–73; Atkin, *Revolution!*, 56–57; Garfías, *Mexican Revolution*, 33; Taracena, *La verdadera revolución*, 1: 120.

25. Atkin, *Revolution!*, 60.

26. Atkin, *Revolution!*, 60.

27. Atkin, *Revolution!*, 65.

28. Beals, *Porfirio Díaz*, 438; Charles C. Cumberland, *Mexican Revolution Genesis under Madero* (Austin: University of Texas Press, 1952), 144.

29. Guzmán, *Memoirs*, 46.

30. Atkin, *Revolution!*, 67; Guzmán, *Memoirs*, 45–46.

31. Atkin, *Revolution!*, 68.

32. Atkin, *Revolution!*, 64–67.

33. Atkin, *Revolution!*, 68–69.

34. Romero, *Anales históricos*, 1: 196–97; Atkin, *Revolution!*, 71; Guzmán, *Memoirs*, 46–47; Taracena, *La verdadera revolución*, 1: 139.

35. Beals, *Porfirio Diaz*, 439; Katz, *Life and Times*, 111–20; Romero, *Anales históricos*, 1: 204; Guzmán, *Memoirs*, 49–50.

36. Quirk, *Mexican Revolution*, 4; Jésus Romero Flores, *Anales Historicos de la revolución mexicana,* 4 vols. (Mexico: El Nacional, 1939), 1: 189–205; Gruening, *Mexico*, 94.

37. Meyer and Sherman, *Course of Mexican History*, 503; Mendoza and Grafías, "El Ejército Mexicano de 1860 a 1913," 275–76; Puente, "Francisco Villa," 1: 249–51; Atkin, *Revolution!*, 83–84, 94–95.

Chapter 2

1. Vasconcelos, *Breve Historia,* 567; Mendoza and Grafías, "El Ejército Mexicano de 1860 a 1913," 336–37; Teja Zabre, *Historia de México* 356–57; Gruening, *Mexico*, 95.

2. Romero, *Anales históricos*, 1: 228–31; Vasconcelos, *Breve Historia* 568–69; Mendoza and Grafías, "El Ejército Mexicano de 1860 a 1913," 338–39; Gutierrez, *Historia militar*, 97–100.
3. Gruening, *Mexico*, 91–92; Romero, *Anales históricos*, 1: 231–33; Mendoza and Grafías, "El Ejército Mexicano de 1860 a 1913," 339–40; Garfías, *Mexican Revolution* 57–59.
4. Guzmán, *Memoirs*, 53–56; Romero, *Anales históricos*, 1: 240–43; Atkin, *Revolution!*, 94–95; Taracena, *La verdadera revolución*, 1: 238.
5. Guzmán, *Memoirs*, 58–59.
6. Atkin, *Revolution!*, 95; Guzmán, *Memoirs*, 59–60; Katz, *Life and Times*, 159–62; Taracena, *La verdadera revolución*, 1: 238.
7. Atkin, *Revolution!*, 96.
8. Romero, *Anales históricos*, 1: 243–45; Mendoza and Grafías, "El Ejército Mexicano de 1860 a 1913," 340–42; Gutierrez, *Historia militar*, 100–108; Krause, *Mexico*, 309.
9. Larry A. Harris, *Pancho Villa and the Columbus Raid* (El Paso: McMath, 1949), 46; Katz, *Life and Times*, 162–65.
10. Romero, *Anales históricos*, 1: 245–47; Krause, *Mexico*, 309; Atkin, *Revolution!*, 98; Guzmán, *Memoirs*, 63–70.
11. Guzmán, *Memoirs*, 73–74; Katz, *Life and Times*, 165–66.
12. Atkin, *Revolution!*, 99.
13. Krause, *Mexico*, 309; Quirk, *Mexican Revolution*, 12–13.
14. Krause, *Mexico*, 309; Quirk, *Mexican Revolution*, 13; Taracena, *La verdadera revolución*, 1: 267; Guzmán, *Memoirs*, 76–80.
15. Romero, *Anales históricos*, 1: 249–51; Garfías, *Mexican Revolution*, 70–71; Beals, *Porfirio Díaz*, 439; Costa Soto, *Historia militar*, 104–105.
16. Guzmán, *Memoirs*, 82.
17. Atkin, *Revolution!*, 101; Guzmán, *Memoirs*, 90.
18. Atkin, *Revolution!*, 101–104; Katz, *Life and Times*, 186–89.
19. Romero, *Anales históricos*, 1: 255–58; Costa Soto, *Historia militar*, 105–106; *Anales gráficos*, 247–49; Romero, *La revolución*, 45.
20. Gutierrez, *Historia militar*, 128–32; Mendoza and Grafías, "El Ejército Mexicano de 1860 a 1913," 351–52; Romero, *Anales históricos*, 1: 258–60; Garfías, *Mexican Revolution*, 73–75.
21. Mendoza and Grafías, "El Ejército Mexicano de 1860 a 1913," 354; Atkin, *Revolution!*, 110–111; Romero, *La revolución*, 46.

22. Matthew Slattery, *Felipe Angeles and the Mexican Revolution* (Dublin, Ind.: PINIT Press, 1982), 44–50; Atkin, *Revolution!*, 111.

23. Quirk, *Mexican Revolution*, 6–7; Vasconcelos, *Breve Historia*, 574–82; Romero, *Anales históricos*, 1: 264–69.

24. Charles C. Cumberland, *Mexican Revolution: The Constitutionalist Years* (Austin: University of Texas Press, 1974), x–xi, 3–10; Vasconcelos, *Breve Historia*, 569.

Chapter 3

1. Cumberland, *Mexican Revolution: Constitutionalist Years*, 28; Quirk, *Mexican Revolution*, 7–8; Atkin, *Revolution!*, 129; Slattery, *Felipe Angeles*, 69.

2. Romero, *Anales históricos*, 2: 8–10; Romero, *La revolución,* 48–49; Grafías, "El Ejército Mexicano de 1913 a 1938," 364.

3. Michael C. Meyer, "The Militarization of Mexico, 1913–1914," *The Americas* 27, no. 3 (January 1971): 293–306; Vasconcelos, *Breve Historia*, 586–87; Garfías, *Mexican Revolution*, 91–95.

4. Cumberland *Mexican Revolution: Constitutionalist Years*, 16, 27; Guzmán, *Memoirs*, 95; Taracena, *La verdadera revolución*, 2: 19; Slattery, *Felipe Angeles*, 56.

5. Guzmán, *Memoirs*, 95.

6. Ramón Puente, *Villa En Pie* (Mexico: Editorial "Mexico Nuevo," 1937), 74.

7. Quirk, *Mexican Revolution*, 15; Cumberland, *Mexican Revolution: Constitutionalist Years*, 70–77; Romero, *Anales históricos*, 2: 19–24; Scott, *Some Memories*, 497.

8. Grafías, "El Ejército Mexicano de 1913 a 1938," 373–75; Garfías, *Mexican Revolution*, 99–100; Costa Soto, *Historia militar*, 108–10; *Anales gráficos*, 275–86.

9. Grafías, "El Ejército Mexicano de 1913 a 1938," 375–77; Garfías, *Mexican Revolution*, 104–105.

10. Taracena, *La verdadera revolución*, 2: 91; Atkin, *Revolution!*, 134; Romero, *Anales históricos*, 2: 29.

11. Guzmán, *Memoirs*, 100–102; Taracena, *La verdadera revolución*, 2: 151; Atkin, *Revolution!*, 147.

12. Atkin, *Revolution!*, 144–46; Katz, *Life and Times*, 259–71.

13. Guzmán, *Memoirs*, 102–105; Katz, *Life and Times*, 216–18; Taracena, *La verdadera revolución*, 2: 153; Atkin, *Revolution!*, 148–49.

14. Guzmán, *Memoirs*, 105; Grafías, "El Ejército Mexicano de 1913 a 1938," 384–86; Atkin, *Revolution!*, 149, 158; Slattery, *Felipe Angeles*, 55–57.

15. Atkin, *Revolution!*, 62, 150.

16. Guzmán, *Memoirs*, 107.

17. Romero, *Anales históricos*, 2: 41–46; Atkin, *Revolution!*, 150; Cumberland, *Mexican Revolution: Constitutionalist Years*, 68.

18. Scott, *Some Memories*, 499; Katz, *Life and Times*, 222–24; Guzmán, *Memoirs*, 107–14; Taracena, *La verdadera revolución*, 2: 171, 178–79.

19. Quirk, *Mexican Revolution*, 17; Krause, *Mexico*, 310; Atkin, *Revolution!*, 160–61; Guzmán, *Memoirs*, 114.

20. Krause, *Mexico*, 310–11; Grafías, "El Ejército Mexicano de 1913 a 1938," 386–88; Atkin, *Revolution!*, 161.

21. I. Thord-Gray, *Gringo Rebel* (Coral Gables: University of Miami Press, 1960) 38; Guzmán, *Memoirs*, 118–19.

22. Guzmán, *Memoirs*, 120.

23. Atkin, *Revolution!*, 162–64; Guzmán, *Memoirs*, 120–21; Thord-Gray, *Gringo Rebel*, 39–47; Taracena, *La verdadera revolución*, 2: 182–83.

24. Thord-Gray, *Gringo Rebel*, 48; Guzmán, *Memoirs*, 122.

25. Cumberland, *Mexican Revolution: Constitutionalist Years*, 50–51; Katz, *Life and Times*, 227–28; Taracena, *La verdadera revolución*, 2: 183.

26. John Reed, *Insurgent Mexico* (New York: International, 1964), 134; Cumberland, *Mexican Revolution: Constitutionalist Years*, 50–51; Guzmán, *Memoirs*, 123–26; Katz, *Life and Times*, 229–31.

27. Reed, *Insurgent Mexico*, 131.

28. Reed, *Insurgent Mexico*, 132–33; Scott, *Some Memories*, 314–15; Atkin, *Revolution!*, 164–65.

29. Atkin, *Revolution!*, 166.

30. Cumberland, *Mexican Revolution: Constitutionalist Years*, 113; Guzmán, *Memoirs*, 126–31; Quirk, *Mexican Revolution*, 17–18; Krause, *Mexico*, 311.

31. Krause, *Mexico*, 312–13; Katz, *Life and Times*, 324–26; Atkin, *Revolution!*, 52.

32. Meyer, "Militarization," 298–300; Meyer and Sherman, *Course of Mexican History*, 525–26; Gutierrez, *Historia militar*, 148–51.

33. Meyer, "Militarization," 302.

34. Quirk, *Mexican Revolution*, 13–14.
35. Thord-Gray, *Gringo Rebel*, 31.
36. Slattery, *Felipe Angeles*, 62.
37. Vasconcelos, *Breve Historia*, 588–89.
38. Slattery, *Felipe Angeles*, 62–63; Quirk, *Mexican Revolution*, 13–14.
39. Slattery, *Felipe Angeles*, 63.
40. Guzmán, *Memoirs*, 132–37; Taracena, *La verdadera revolución*, 2: 221; Atkin, *Revolution!*, 169–73; Katz, *Life and Times*, 326–30.
41. Atkin, *Revolution!*, 176.
42. Quirk, *Mexican Revolution*, 19.
43. Cumberland, *Mexican Revolution: Constitutionalist Years*, 35–36; Quirk, *Mexican Revolution*, 20; Atkin, *Revolution!*, 178.
44. Quirk, *Mexican Revolution*, 20; Slattery, *Felipe Angeles*, 71.
45. Slattery, *Felipe Angeles*, 70–71; Atkin, *Revolution!*, 179; Taracena, *La verdadera revolución*, 2: 232.
46. Quirk, *Mexican Revolution*, 21–22; Slattery, *Felipe Angeles*, 71; Cumberland, *Mexican Revolution: Constitutionalist Years*, 117; Guzmán, *Memoirs*, 148–51.
47. Quirk, *Mexican Revolution*, 22.
48. Quirk, *Mexican Revolution*, 23; Atkin, *Revolution!*, 180; Taracena, *La verdadera revolución*, 2: 235–36.
49. Slattery, *Felipe Angeles*, 72–73; Guzmán, *Memoirs*, 156–63; Atkin, *Revolution!*, 180–81.
50. Slattery, *Felipe Angeles*, 73.
51. Atkin, *Revolution!*, 181–82; Guzmán, *Memoirs*, 164–67.
52. Rafael F. Muñoz, *Vámonos con Pancho Villa* (Mexico: Espasa-Calpe Argentina, 1950), 108–11.
53. Slattery, *Felipe Angeles*, 74; Guzmán, *Memoirs*, 179–81; Katz, *Life and Times*, 306–308; Taracena, *La verdadera revolución*, 2: 242.
54. Atkin, *Revolution!*, 184; Guzmán, *Memoirs*, 180.
55. Krause, *Mexico*, 313; Quirk, *Mexican Revolution*, 24; Reed, *Insurgent Mexico*, 140.
56. Quirk, *Mexican Revolution*, 26–27; Juan Barragán Rodríguez, *Historia del ejército y de la revolución constitutionalista*, 2 vols. (Mexico: Comisión nacional para las celebraciones del 175 aniversario de la independencia nacional . . . , 1985) 1: 373–419.
57. Barragán, *Historia*, 1: 438–47; Cumberland, *Mexican Revolution: Constitutionalist Years*, 129–31; Quirk, *Mexican Revolution*, 25.
58. Quirk, *Mexican Revolution*, 26.

59. Cumberland, *Mexican Revolution: Constitutionalist Years*, 119; Guzmán, *Memoirs*, 185–88; Quirk, *Mexican Revolution*, 26; Costa Soto, *Historia military*, 116–17, 269, 287.

60. Barragán, *Historia*, 1: 432–38.

61. Slattery, *Felipe Angeles*, 75–76; Costa Soto, *Historia military*, 115; Romero, *La revolución*, 55–56.

62. Cumberland, *Mexican Revolution: Constitutionalist Years*, 124–25; Taracena, *La verdadera revolución*, 2: 252–53; Romero, *Anales históricos*, 2: 54–56.

63. Costa Soto, *Historia militar*, 117–18; Grafías, "El Ejército Mexicano de 1913 a 1938," 342; Garfías, *Mexican Revolution*, 117–18; *Anales gráficos*, 331–38.

64. Barragán, *Historia*, 1: 469–92.

65. Barragán, *Historia*, 1: 509–15; Guzmán, *Memoirs*, 191–93; Krause, *Mexico*, 314.

66. Guzmán, *Memoirs*, 197.

67. Krause, *Mexico*, 314; Slattery, *Felipe Angeles*, 85–87; Cumberland, *Mexican Revolution: Constitutionalist Years*, 122; Taracena, *La verdadera revolución*, 2: 267–68.

68. Guzmán, *Memoirs*, 199.

69 Atkin, *Revolution!*, 204–205

70. Cumberland, *Mexican Revolution: Constitutionalist Years*, 135; Slattery, *Felipe Angeles*, 97–99; Taracena, *La verdadera revolución*, 2: 279–80.

71. Guzmán, *Memoirs*, 214; Taracena, *La verdadera revolución*, 2: 283–85.

72. Guzmán, *Memoirs*, 220; Taracena, *La verdadera revolución*, 2: 285–87.

73. Barragán, *Historia*, 1: 537–40; Slattery, *Felipe Angeles*, 99–101.

74. Slattery, *Felipe Angeles*, 107–108; Guzmán, *Memoirs*, 222–27.

75. Barragán, *Historia*, 1: 559.

76. Slattery, *Felipe Angeles*, 111–13; Guzmán, *Memoirs*, 228–41; Katz, *Life and Times*, 348–53; Garfías, *Mexican Revolution*, 123–24; Taracena, *La verdadera revolución*, 2: 289–90.

77. Atkin, *Revolution!*, 207.

78. Romero, *Anales históricos*, 2: 53–54; Cumberland, *Mexican Revolution: Constitutionalist Years*, 140; Slattery, *Felipe Angeles*, 115–17.

79. Barragán, *Historia*, 1: 539–42; Atkin, *Revolution!*, 207.

80. Slattery, *Felipe Angeles*, 116.
81. Quirk, *Mexican Revolution*, 38–40.
82. Quirk, *Mexican Revolution*, 40–41.
83. Guzmán, *Memoirs*, 249–58; Quirk, *Mexican Revolution*, 41–43;
    Taracena, *La verdadera revolución*, 2: 296–98.
84. Guzmán, *Memoirs*, 258–61; Slattery, *Felipe Angeles*, 117; Atkin,
    Revolution!, 208.
85. Romero, *Anales históricos*, 2: 69–70; Grafías, "El Ejército
    Mexicano de 1913 a 1938," 397–99; Garfías, *Mexican Revolution*,
    126; *Anales gráficos*, 339, 345.
86. José Vasconcelos, *La Tormenta* (Mexico: Editorial Trillas, 1998),
    70.

Chapter 4

1. Cumberland, *Mexican Revolution: Constitutionalist Years*, 149–50;
   Taracena, *La verdadera revolución*, 2: 330.
2. Quirk, *Mexican Revolution*, 44; Barragán, *Historia*, 1: 581; Atkin,
   Revolution!, 213.
3. Cumberland, *Mexican Revolution: Constitutionalist Years*, 151–54;
   Guzmán, *Memoirs*, 288–300; Slattery, *Felipe Angeles*, 117–18.
4. Alvaro Obregón, *Ocho mil kilómetros en campaña*, 2 vols.
   (Mexico: Editorial del Valle de Mexico, S.A. de CV, 1980), 1:
   284.
5. Krause, *Mexico*, 322.
6. Cumberland, *Mexican Revolution: Constitutionalist Years*, 154–56;
   Barragán, *Historia*, 2: 68–73; Guzmán, *Memoirs*, 288–304;
   Taracena, *La verdadera revolución*, 3: 20.
7. Obregón, *Ocho mil kilómetros*, 330.
8. Obregón, *Ocho mil kilómetros*, 1: 332; Cumberland, *Mexican
   Revolution: Constitutionalist Years*, 156–57, Guzmán, *Memoirs*,
   309–18; Slattery, *Felipe Angeles*, 118.
9. Quirk, *Mexican Revolution*, 78–79; Romero, *Anales históricos*, 2:
   84–86.
10. Barragán, *Historia*, 2: 83–87; Cumberland, *Mexican Revolution:
    Constitutionalist Years*, 158–59.
11. Quirk, *Mexican Revolution*, 79.
12. Quirk, *Mexican Revolution*, 80.
13. Quirk, *Mexican Revolution*, 80–82; Obregón, *Ocho mil
    kilométros*, 2: 283–97; Katz, *Life and Times*, 368–71; Atkin,

Revolution!, 219–20.

14. Atkin, *Revolution!*, 220; Cumberland, *Mexican Revolution: Constitutionalist Years*, 165–66; Guzmán, *Memoirs*, 321–23; Taracena, *La verdadera revolución*, 3: 42.

15. Vasconcelos, *La Tormenta*, 104; Katz, *Life and Times*, 374–75.

16. Katz, *Life and Times*, 373–74; Quirk, *Mexican Revolution*, 82–85.

17. Vasconcelos, *La Tormenta*, 101–102.

18. Cumberland, *Mexican Revolution: Constitutionalist Years*, 170; Quirk, *Mexican Revolution*, 101–106; Romero, *Anales históricos*, 2: 92–95; Guzmán, *Memoirs*, 324–27.

19. Quirk, *Mexican Revolution*, 106–107; Slattery, *Felipe Angeles*, 120–21; Atkin, *Revolution!*, 223.

20. Cumberland, *Mexican Revolution: Constitutionalist Years*, 172–73; Quirk, *Mexican Revolution*, 112–13; Slattery, *Felipe Angeles*, 121–22.

21. Vasconcelos, *La Tormenta*, 123–39; Quirk, *Mexican Revolution*, 115; Guzmán, *Memoirs*, 339–43.

22. Vasconcelos, *La Tormenta*, 139–44; Romero, *Anales históricos*, 2: 96–97; Quirk, *Mexican Revolution*, 118–19; Cumberland, *Mexican Revolution: Constitutionalist Years*, 173–74.

23. Quirk, *Mexican Revolution*, 123–34; Cumberland, *Mexican Revolution: Constitutionalist Years*, 177–82; Slattery, *Felipe Angeles*, 126; Atkin, *Revolution!*, 228.

24. Quirk, *Mexican Revolution*, 134; Atkin, *Revolution!*, 230.

25. Quirk, *Mexican Revolution*, 139–40; Atkin, *Revolution!*, 215; Katz, *Life and Times*, 435–36; Taracena, *La verdadera revolución*, 3: 106–107.

26. Guzmán, *Memoirs*, 375–78; Quirk, *Mexican Revolution*, 140.

27. "Pacto de Xochimilco," in Manuel González Ramírez, *Fuentes para la historia del la revolución mexicana: planes políticos y otros documentos*, 4 vols. (Mexico: Fondo de Cultura Económica, 1954–57), 1: 115, 119.

28. Cumberland, *Mexican Revolution: Constitutionalist Years*, 183–85; Guzmán, *Memoirs*, 378–82; Taracena, *La verdadera revolución*, 3: 110.

29. Slattery, *Felipe Angeles*, 128–29, 140–41; Atkin, *Revolution!*, 235.

30. Cumberland, *Mexican Revolution: Constitutionalist Years*, 187.

31. Vasconcelos, *La Tormenta*, 152–56; Cumberland, *Mexican Revolution: Constitutionalist Years*, 185; Johnson, *Heroic Mexico*,

270; Atkin, *Revolution!*, 236.

32. Cumberland, *Mexican Revolution: Constitutionalist Years*, 186–87; Quirk, *Mexican Revolution*, 141–42; Atkin, *Revolution!*, 234.

33. Cumberland, *Mexican Revolution: Constitutionalist Years*, 188–89; Quirk, *Mexican Revolution*, 143.

34. Quirk, *Mexican Revolution*, 162.

35. Scott, *Some Memories*, 509–10; Guzmán, *Memoirs*, 400–404, 410–14.

36. Krause, *Mexico*, 325–26.

37. Romero, *Anales históricos*, 2: 103–107; Taracena, *La verdadera revolución*, 3: 134–35.

38. Barragán, *Historia*, 2: 175–77; Cumberland, *Mexican Revolution: Constitutionalist Years*, 187–88; Atkin, *Revolution!*, 240.

39. Romero, *Anales históricos*, 2: 109–11; Barragán, *Historia*, 2: 177; Quirk, *Mexican Revolution*, 166–75; Guzmán, *Memoirs*, 405–409, 415–19.

40. Cumberland, *Mexican Revolution: Constitutionalist Years*, 192–93; Guzmán, *Memoirs*, 429–34; Slattery, *Felipe Angeles*, 140–41.

41. Atkin, *Revolution!*, 249; Romero, *Anales históricos*, 2: 113–14; Taracena, *La verdadera revolución*, 3: 152–53.

42. Atkin, *Revolution!*, 250; Guzmán, *Memoirs*, 434–42; Taracena, *La verdadera revolución*, 3: 186–87.

43. Barragán, *Historia* 2: 211–12; Taracena, *La verdadera revolución*, 3: 168.

44. Slattery, *Felipe Angeles*, 142; Atkin, *Revolution!*, 241.

45. Cumberland, *Mexican Revolution: Constitutionalist Years*, 193–94; Quirk, *Mexican Revolution*, 180–84; Atkin, *Revolution!*, 242.

46. Cumberland, *Mexican Revolution: Constitutionalist Years*, 196; Slattery, *Felipe Angeles*, 142–43; Romero, *Anales históricos*, 2: 116–17; Costa Soto, *Historia militar*, 124.

47. Atkin, *Revolution!*, 243; Cumberland, *Mexican Revolution: Constitutionalist Years*, 194–96.

48. Slattery, *Felipe Angeles*, 143; Atkin, *Revolution!*, 242–44; Taracena, *La verdadera revolución*, 3: 181.

49. Slattery, *Felipe Angeles*, 137–38.

50. Taracena, *La verdadera revolución*, 3: 209; Atkin, *Revolution!*, 250.

51. Manuel W. González, *Contra Villa* (Mexico: Ediciones Botas, 1935), 129–33; Cumberland, *Mexican Revolution: Constitutionalist Years*, 200.

52. Guzmán, *Memoirs*, 446–48; Slattery, *Felipe Angeles*, 140–41; Taracena, *La verdadera revolución*, 3: 186; Atkin, *Revolution!*, 250.

53. Romero, *Anales históricos*, 2: 120–21; Guzmán, *Memoirs*, 449–52; Costa Soto, *Historia militar*, 125; Garfías, *Mexican Revolution*, 142.

54. Slattery, *Felipe Angeles*, 138.

55. Quirk, *Mexican Revolution*, 220–21.

56. Slattery, *Felipe Angeles*, 143.

57. Barragán, *Historia*, 2: 297–80; Taracena, *La verdadera revolución*, 3: 229; Grafías, "El Ejército Mexicano de 1913 a 1938," 408.

58. Obregón, *Ocho mil kilómetros*, 2: 518–19; Garfías, *Mexican Revolution*, 145–47; Grafías, "El Ejército Mexicano de 1913 a 1938," 409.

59. Quirk, *Mexican Revolution*, 222; Slattery, *Felipe Angeles*, 144; Taracena, *La verdadera revolución*, 3: 229–31.

60. Obregón, *Ocho mil kilómetros*, 2: 521.

61. Grafías, "El Ejército Mexicano de 1913 a 1938," 411–12; Slattery, *Felipe Angeles*, 143–44; Atkin, *Revolution!*, 250–51; Guzmán, *Memoirs*, 456–59.

62. Barragán, *Historia*, 2: 280–85; Atkin, *Revolution!*, 251.

63. Romero, *Anales históricos*, 2: 129–43; Grafías, "El Ejército Mexicano de 1913 a 1938," 413–15; Guzmán, *Memoirs*, 464–66; Cumberland, *Mexican Revolution: Constitutionalist Years*, 200–201.

64. Guzmán, *Memoirs*, 480; Barragán, *Historia*, 2: 322–55; Quirk, *Mexican Revolution*, 261.

65. Slattery, *Felipe Angeles*, 146–47.

66. Slattery, *Felipe Angeles*, 147–48.

67. Slattery, *Felipe Angeles*, 148; Taracena, *La verdadera revolución*, 3: 252–53.

68. Slattery, *Felipe Angeles*, 149.

69. John W. F. Dulles, *Yesterday in Mexico* (Austin: University of Texas Press, 1972), 12–13; Slattery, *Felipe Angeles*, 149; Romero, *Anales históricos*, 2: 145.

70. Slattery, *Felipe Angeles*, 149–50; Taracena, *La verdadera revolución*, 3: 286–87.

71. Romero, *Anales históricos*, 2: 143–47; Barragán, *Historia* 2: 344–48; Slattery, *Felipe Angeles*, 150; Quirk, *Mexican Revolution*, 225; Cumberland, *Mexican Revolution: Constitutionalist Years*, 202–203.

72. Grafías, "El Ejército Mexicano de 1913 a 1938," 416–17; Garfías, *Mexican Revolution,* 155–56; Slattery, *Felipe Angeles,* 157; Cumberland, *Mexican Revolution: Constitutionalist Years,* 203.

73. United States, *Foreign Relations, 1915* (Washington: Government Printing Office, 1916), 724; Romero, *Anales históricos,* 2: 175–76.

74. Romero, *Anales históricos,* 2: 168–70, 176–78; González, *Contra Villa,* 342–49.

75. Romero, *Anales históricos,* 2: 172–73, 178–79.

76. Krause, *Mexico,* 328.

77. Krause, *Mexico,* 326.

Chapter 5

1. Quirk, *Mexican Revolution,* 283–84.

2. Krause, *Mexico,* 327; Atkin, *Revolution!,* 254.

3. Krause, *Mexico,* 327–28.

4. Romero, *Anales históricos,* 2: 183–92; Taracena, *La verdadera revolución,* 4: 98–101; Atkin, *Revolution!,* 265–66.

5. Atkin, *Revolution!,* 266; Taracena, *La verdadera revolución,* 4: 101–102.

6. Atkin, *Revolution!,* 267.

7. Taracena, *La verdadera revolución,* 4: 104–107; Atkin, *Revolution!,* 267; Romero, *Anales históricos,* 2: 192–93; Krause, *Mexico,* 328.

8. Atkin, *Revolution!,* 267.

9. Katz, *Life and Times,* 557–60; Taracena, *La verdadera revolución,* 4: 121–22; Atkin, *Revolution!,* 269–71; Romero, *Anales históricos,* 2: 203–204.

10. Atkin, *Revolution!,* 272.

11. Taracena, *La verdadera revolución,* 4: 153–55; Atkin, *Revolution!,* 275–78; Romero, *Anales históricos,* 2: 207–208.

12. Atkin, *Revolution!,* 278–79.

13. Romero, *Anales históricos,* 2: 208–11.

14. Thomas F. Burdett, "Mobilization of 1911 and 1913," *Military Review,* no. 7, 65–74 (July 1974).

15. Atkin, *Revolution!,* 280–81

16. James A. Houston, *The Sinews of War: Army Logistics, 1775–1953* (Washington: Center for Military History, 1988), 298–99, 305; Atkin, *Revolution!,* 282.

17. Atkin, *Revolution!,* 282–83.

18. Atkin, *Revolution!*, 283–84; Taracena, *La verdadera revolución*, 4: 165.
19. Atkin, *Revolution!*, 284; Romero, *Anales históricos*, 2: 212–13.
20. Romero, *Anales históricos*, 2: 214–15; Taracena, *La verdadera revolución*, 4: 169–70; Atkin, *Revolution!*, 284–85.
21. Scott, *Some Memories*, 525–28; Romero, *Anales históricos*, 2: 216; Atkin, *Revolution!*, 285–86.
22. Atkin, *Revolution!*, 287–88.
23. Taracena, *La verdadera revolución*, 4: 199–200; Romero, *Anales históricos*, 2: 212–21; Atkin, *Revolution!*, 288–89.
24. Romero, *Anales históricos*, 2: 221–24; Taracena, *La verdadera revolución*, 4: 202; Atkin, *Revolution!*, 289–90.
25. Krause, *Mexico,* 329; Atkin, *Revolution!*, 290–91; Romero, *La revolución,* 68–69.
26. Taracena, *La verdadera revolución*, 5: 33; Cumberland, *Mexican Revolution: Constitutionalist Years*, 324–25; Atkin, *Revolution!*, 291.
27. Romero, *Anales históricos*, 2: 224
28. Atkin, *Revolution!*, 304.
29. Atkin, *Revolution!*, 304–305.
30. Taracena, *La verdadera revolución*, 5: 181.
31. Atkin, *Revolution!*, 305–306.
32. Slattery, *Felipe Angeles,* 175.
33. Slattery, *Felipe Angeles,* 175; Taracena, *La verdadera revolución*, 5: 102.
34. Taracena, *La verdadera revolución*, 5: 115–16; Krause, *Mexico,* 330–31.
35. E. J. Dillon, *Mexico on the Verge* (London: Hutchinson, 1922), 18; Taracena, *La verdadera revolución,* 6: 202.

Chapter 6

1. Cumberland, *Mexican Revolution: Constitutionalist Years,* 320–60.
2. Vasconcelos, *Breve Historia,* 615–16; Romero, *Anales históricos*, 2: 281–302; Cumberland, *Mexican Revolution: Constitutionalist Years,* 404–406.
3. Dulles, *Yesterday,* 33, 65–66.
4. Dulles, *Yesterday,* 67–68.

5. Romero, *Anales históricos*, 3: 10–11; Atkin, *Revolution!*, 318; Cumberland, *Mexican Revolution: Constitutionalist Years*, 412–17.
6. Atkin, *Revolution!*, 318–19.
7. Atkin, *Revolution!*, 319–20; Dulles, *Yesterday*, 67–69; Krause, *Mexico*, 332;, *La verdadera revolución*, 7: 49–50.
8. Atkin, *Revolution!*, 320;, *La verdadera revolución*, 7: 56–61.
9. Romero, *Anales históricos*, 3: 14–16.
10. Dulles, *Yesterday*, 69–70; Atkin, *Revolution!*, 323.
11. Reed, *Insurgent Mexico*, 145; Dulles, *Yesterday*, 178.
12. Atkin, *Revolution!*, 323; Reed, *Insurgent Mexico*, 144–45.
13. Atkin, *Revolution!*, 323.
14. Dulles, *Yesterday*, 177–78; Atkin, *Revolution!*, 324.
15. Dulles, *Yesterday*, 179–80; Atkin, *Revolution!*, 324.
16. Dulles, *Yesterday*, 180; Atkin, *Revolution!*, 324.
17. Scott, *Some Memories*, 518.

Chapter 7
1. Vasconcelos, *La Tormenta*, 82
2. Kirkpatrick, *Latin America,* 349; Harold Davis, *History of Latin America* (New York: Ronald Press, 968), 618; Slattery, *Felipe Angeles*, xi.
3. Reed, *Insurgent Mexico*, 234.
4. Puente, "Francisco Villa," 1: 243.
5. Louis Stevens, *Here Comes Pancho Villa* (New York: Frederick A. Stokes, 1930), 90.
6. Scott, *Some Memories*, 501.
7. Krause, *Mexico*, 318.
8. Reed, *Insurgent Mexico*, 133; Peterson and Knoles, *Pancho Villa*, xi; Krause, *Mexico*, 321.
9. Scott, *Some Memories*, 515.
10. Krause, *Mexico*, 316.
11. Reed, *Insurgent Mexico*, 139; Scott, *Some Memories*, 507.
12. Thord-Gray, *Rebel Gringo*, 30.
13. Reed, *Insurgent Mexico*, 143.
14. Peterson and Knoles, *Pancho Villa*, 28.
15. Peterson and Knoles, *Pancho Villa*, 261.
16. Atkin, *Revolution!*, 146.
17. Thord-Gray, *Rebel Gringo*, 33.

18. Krause, *Mexico*, 316.
19. Quirk, *Mexican Revolution*, 82–83.
20. Scott, *Some Memories*, 516.
21. Atkin, *Revolution!*, 175.
22. Krause, *Mexico*, 316.
23. Scott, *Some Memories*, 518.

Bibliographic Notes

(See endnotes for full citations of works cited in this section.)

This bibliographic essay is written to those individuals who are interested in Pancho Villa as a soldier and those who are interested in the military aspects of the fighting in northern Mexico during the Revolution.

First, I suggest that you read at least one of the numerous survey histories of this ten-year conflict. The following were most useful to me: Ronald Atkin, *Revolution!*; Luis Grafías M., *The Mexican Revolution*; and Robert E. Quirk, *The Mexican Revolution.*

Next, there are numerous military histories of the revolution that provide much insight, most of which are in Spanish. The ones that I found most useful for the fighting in northern Mexico were Juan Barragán, *Historia*; Alvaro Obregón, *Ocho mil kilómetros*; Jesús Romero Flores, *Anales históricos*; and Matthew Slatter, *Felipe Angeles.*

First-hand accounts of the fighting, particularly that in northern Mexico, were important for understanding Villa's world. For me, the most useful were John Kenneth Turner, *Barbarous Mexico*, and Timothy G. Turner, *Bullets.*

Within revolutionary Mexico, to rise to significant command, you had to raise and sustain a large following. Therefore, to evaluate Villa as a military commander, you need to understand Villa the man. I found the writings of those who knew Villa to be crucial. The accounts that I found most revealing were Ramón Puente, "Francisco Villa"; I. Thord-Gray, *Gringo*

Rebel; John Reed, *Insurgent Mexico*; Hugh Lenox Scott, *Some Memories*; and José Vasconcelos, *La Tormenta*.

Last are the writings of Pancho Villa himself that may be found in Martín Luis Guzmán, *Memoirs*, and numerous interviews published in newspapers and elsewhere.

Index

About the Author

Robert L. Scheina, Ph.D., spent twelve years on the faculty at the National Defense University as a professor of history and has lectured at senior military colleges throughout the Western Hemisphere. He currently teaches at the Inter-American Defense College. A leading authority on Latin American history, his previous books include *Latin America's Wars* (Vols. I & II), *Latin America: A Naval History, 1810–1987*, and *Santa Anna: A Curse Upon Mexico*, a volume in Brassey's Military Profiles Series. He lives in the Washington, D.C., area.

MILITARY PROFILES
AVAILABLE

Farragut: America's First Admiral
Robert J. Schneller, Jr.

Drake: For God, Queen, and Plunder
Wade G. Dudley

Santa Anna: A Curse upon Mexico
Robert L. Scheina

Eisenhower: Soldier-Statesman of the American Century
Douglas Kinnard

Semmes: Rebel Raider
John M. Taylor

Doolittle: Aerospace Visionary
Dik Alan Daso

Foch: Supreme Allied Commander in the Great War
Michael S. Neiberg

Villa: Soldier of the Mexican Revolution
Robert L. Scheina

Cushing: Civil War SEAL
Robert J. Schneller, Jr.

Alexander the Great: Invincible King of Macedonia
Peter G. Tsouras

MILITARY PROFILES
FORTHCOMING
Meade
Richard A. Sauers
Halsey
Robert J. Cressman
Rickover
Thomas B. Allen/Norman Polmar
Tirpitz
Michael Epkenhans